M000164521

Three names for a single city: known as Byzantium, Constantinople and Istanbul, the three names signify whole worlds that could hardly be more different from one another, more confusing or more seductive. Different, because the "clash" or the "meeting" of two cultures here is more than a cliché; it is part of everyday life. Confusing, because the city beguiles all the visitor's senses. Seductive, because you cannot help but fall in love with the city. The gateway between East and West, the city likes to change its apperance but it never loses face. At the present time, it undergoes a period of profound and deep-seated change, from UNESCO World Heritage Site with a grand past via an exciting present to European capital and to its irresistible rise as a future economic world city. And yet the "city of a hundred names" will remain what it has always been: the ever-shining beauty of the Bosphorus.

InGuide Istanbul is illustrated with stunning photographs as you would expect to find in a large coffeetable book yet it is also a highly informative travel guide book. District by district, lots of images and vivid descriptions introduce all the sights, revealing many amazing facts about the city and its people, about art and culture, about the everyday and the unusual. In "Compact Istanbul", insider tips point out the best restaurants, hotels and shops, as well as the trendy neighborhoods, important addresses, and useful facts. Another chapter introduces all the top museums with detailed information and photographs. Finally, the City Walks are packed with shopping and dining tips that will inspire you to explore all of the Istanbul districts and areas. A detailed, removable city map completes this unique picture travel guide. It makes it easy for you to find all the city's highlights by grid reference.

CONTENTS

Napoleon once said, "If the world were a single state then its capital would be Constantinople". Left: the historic Old Town with the Hagia Sophia (on the left) and the Sultan Ahmet Mosque. Previous pages: a roof restaurant in Sultanahmet; Ortaköy at the foot of the First Bosphorus Bridge and in the background Şişli.

View of the Sultan Ahmed Mosque and the city's sea of lights: "I hear Istanbul, my eyes closed. / A light breeze at first, / Gently swaying / The leaves in the trees … " (Orhan Veli Kanık)

THIS SIDE OF THE GOLDEN HORN: THE OLD TOWN AND EYÜP

Alongside Rome and Jerusalem, Istanbul is one of the oldest cities in the world. Like Rome, Istanbul was built on seven hills and like Jerusalem, it has played a key role in the history of the world's religions. The location of the Old Town, now a UNESCO World Heritage Site, on a peninsula between Golden Horn, Bosphorus and Sea of Marmara, is unparalleled, however. On the landside to the west, outside the ancient city walls, is the Eyüp district (named after one of Mohammed's standard bearers) with the Eyüp Sultan Mosque – the most important pilgrimage site for Turkish Muslims after Mecca, Medina and Jerusalem.

THIS SIDE OF THE GOLDEN HORN: THE OLD TOWN AND EYÜP

Situated in the Old Town's loveliest spot where the eastern tip of the peninsula extends into the Bosphorus, the Topkapi Palace was built by Sultan Mehmed II (1432–1481) after his conquest of Constantinople, which signaled the end of the Byzantine Empire (1453). Initially planned as an administrative center, the palace was the official seat of government of the Ottoman Empire under Suleiman I (c. 1494–1566). The centuries that followed saw it develop into a feudal palace complex grouped around four large courtyards and comprising mosques, baths, kitchens, libraries, residential quarters

and gardens. The name Topkapı ("cannon gate") refers to an earlier artillery position on the peninsula. In 1856 the leaders of the government, administration and military – more than 5,000 people in all – moved into the new Dolmabahçe Palace, leaving only the national mint in the Topkapı Palace.

The palace complex (large picture and top), covering around 70 ha (173 acres) and enclosed by a wall with 28 towers, is spread across the ancient acropolis in the Byzantion of old (the name of the Greek colony founded on the Bosphorus in c. 660 BC). It has been open to the public since 1924. Above: The Shahadah, the name of the Islamic creed, as a calligraphic decoration in the state council (divan) assembly room.

The treasury in the Topkapı Palace was built under Sultan Bayezid II (c. 1447–1512), after an earthquake in 1509 had destroyed an earlier pavilion of Mehmed II on the same site. The sultans initially stored their private treasures here in the underground vaults, while audiences were held in the rooms above. It was his son, Sultan Selim I (1470–1520), who first declared the whole wing to be the treasury. Gifts to the sultans as well as the spoils of their wars were hoarded here, including the holiest of Islamic reliquaries brought back to Istanbul by Selim I in 1517 following his Egyptian campaign and which is today on view in the Topkapı Palace reliquary collection: Mohammed's cloak, a bronze panel with his footprint and hair from the prophet's beard. On display in the treasury itself are thrones decorated with ivory and mother-of-pearl and a gold-plated wooden twig for

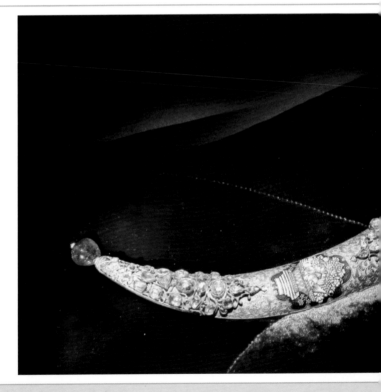

THE POWER AND THE GLORY OF THE OTTOMAN RULERS: INSIDE THE TREASURY

the princes who were born in the palace, as well as valuables such as the legendary, jewel-studded Topkapı Emerald Dagger, which Sultan Mahmud I (1696–1754) had made for the Shah of Persia, and the 86-carat "Spoonmaker's Diamond", the fourth largest in the world, framed by 49 gemstones.

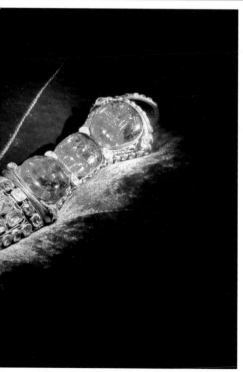

Three large emeralds glisten on the handle of the Topkapı Dagger (left). The dagger remained in the sultan's possession because the recipient of the decorative weapon was murdered before the gift could be presented to him. The Spoonmaker's Diamond (above), alleged to have been found in a rubbish heap and exchanged at a spoonmaker's, is one of the main attractions in the treasury (top: a detail of the entrance portal).

The Topkapı Palace's harem was a "city within a city". Black eunuchs, under penalty of death, were responsible for ensuring that no man other than the sultan himself entered this forbidden realm ("haram" is the Arabic word for "forbidden"). Here hundreds of concubines vied for the ruler's attention and for the privilege of bearing him a son. In contrast to the West's romantic image, however, a harem was more like a convent than a love nest, with strict rules and a clearly defined hierarchy. The larger and more luxurious the rooms, the higher the status of the occupants. The most powerful position was generally held by the *valide sultan*, the sultan's mother. She lived like a princess holding her own court and had the last word when it came to wives and concubines, spoilt favorites and oppressed slaves. Not only did she assist her son in the selection of his concubines, it was also not

The harem in the Topkapı Palace is a winding labyrinth of more than 300 rooms linked via courtyards, stairs and corridors (above). In the harem's banquet and throne room (right) the women passed their time with dancing, music and drama performances. The forbidden realm also caught the imagination of European artists: this portrayal of new mothers in the harem (top right) was painted by Jean-Baptiste Vanmour in 1720.

uncommon for her to advise him on issues of government as well. It was no wonder then that members of the harem who had borne the sultan a prince made every effort to assume this position themselves as quickly as possible – leading to a great deal of intrigue and even murder.

THIS SIDE OF THE GOLDEN HORN:
THE OLD TOWN AND EYÜP

One of the city's oldest surviving religious buildings from ancient Byzantium is the church of the "Holy Peace" (Greek: Hagia Eirene). The aura of peace and tranquility did not prevent the Janissaries from using the church as an armory, however. The Hagia Eirene stands in the first outer courtyard of the Topkapı Palace, the domain of the Janissaries, an elite unit within the Ottoman Empire from amongst whom the sultan's bodyguards were also recruited. The church is thought to have been built in around the year AD 300, on the site of an Aphrodite sanctuary. The First Council of Constan-

Declared a museum in 1948, today the Hagia Eirene is open to the public only for by special permission or for events (right: a concert by the Istanbul State Symphony Orchestra; above: the apse decorated with a cross against a gold background). The oldest surviving sections of the domed basilica (on the right-hand edge of the picture top right) date from the 6th century when the church was rebuilt following devastation by a fire.

tinople (also known as the Second Ecumenical Council) met here in 381 under the East Roman Emperor Theodosius I. Attended by 150 bishops, this council formulated the Christian Niceno-Constantinopolitan creed still in use today. The church is now a museum and hall for classical concerts.

THIS SIDE OF THE GOLDEN HORN:
THE OLD TOWN AND EYÜP

Somewhat hidden between the Topkapı Palace and Gülhane Park, formerly the palace gardens, is the Archaeological Museum founded in 1896 by the Turkish archaeologist and painter Osman Hamdi Bey (1842–1910). It houses three first-class collections: the Museum of the Ancient Orient in the building constructed in 1883 as an art academy, to the left side of the entrance; the Museum of Islamic Art housed in the Tiled Kiosk (Çinili Köşk) built outside of the palace grounds in 1472 and the Archaeological Museum in the three wings of the neoclassical main building. The latter holds

valuable sarcophagi as one of the museum's highlights. They were discovered during excavations led by the museum's founder Hamdi Bey in the Sidon necropolis, a Phoenician port city conquered by Alexander the Great in 332 BC on the site of present-day Sidon in southern Lebanon.

The Alexander Sarcophagus from Sidon (c. 330 BC) does not contain the remains of Alexander the Great but portrays his deeds with impressive carvings. On the left he is depicted as the aggressor in the Battle of Issus (333 BC). Together with the Sarcophagus of the Crying Women (above, 4th C. BC), also from Sidon, it is one of the museum's most important exhibits. Top: the sculpture of a young athlete (1st C.) in the Ephebe Room.

THIS SIDE OF THE GOLDEN HORN:
THE OLD TOWN AND EYÜP

One of the loveliest Turkish rococo fountains is located directly in front of the entrance to the first of the Topkapı Palace courtyards: with its five attractive little domes and the wavy, overhanging roof, the charming bay windows with their bronze bars, the Fountain of Sultan Ahmed is more evocative of a villa or a small palace than a drinking fountain. Its appealing bay windows and the luxuriant floral motifs on the walls simply reinforce the impression of its amazing grandeur. The fountain was commissioned in 1728 by Sultan Ahmed III (1673–1736) and built solely

"Drink this water and say a prayer for Sultan Ahmed", reads the inscription in Arabic lettering on the fountain building. The walls feature verses from the poet Seyit Vehbi (c. 1674–1734), in which the quality of the water is held to be "paradisiacal". Vehbi's close relationship to the sultan is also documented by his main work, the Surnâme-i Vehbî festival book, in which the poet recounts the circumcision festival of the sultan's sons.

for mundane purposes, however, namely to provide thirsty passers-by with aromatic drinking water and sorbets. The fountain's floral decoration is highly typical of the era in which it was built, the so-called "Tulip Period" (1718–1730) being symbolic of both subtlety and playfulness.

THIS SIDE OF THE GOLDEN HORN:
THE OLD TOWN AND EYÜP

Istanbul was known as Constantinople from 330 to 1930. It enjoyed its golden age as the capital of the Byzantine Empire after being founded by the Emperor Constantine the Great. The city's best-known building is the Hagia Sophia, a palatial church commissioned by Emperor Justinian the Great. It was built between 532 and 537 by Isidore of Miletus on the site of the ruined basilica completed by Constantine in 360. The Hagia Sophia remained the main church of the Byzantine Empire for more than 900 years and the central mosque of the Ottoman Empire for almost 500 years, the

church having been converted to a mosque following the Ottoman conquest of the city in 1453. At that time the mosaics were covered over with plaster and a number of new buildings added to the complex, including the four minarets. The Hagia Sophia has been a museum since 1934.

The Hagia Sophia, the most important example of Byzantine architecture, combines a nave section with a domed main building. Once the coronation church of the Byzantine emperors, it is dominated by the main dome (32.2 m/106 ft diameter, crown height 56.2 m/184 ft) on the main axis, supported by two half domes each with three auxiliary domes, supplemented by a series of two-floor domes to the north and the south.

Only the best of materials were good enough for the construction of the Hagia Sophia: silver and gold work from Ephesus, for example; ophicalcite, a crystal limestone, from Thessaly; and white marble from the Marmara Islands. Luminous mosaics used to cover an area of around 16,000 sq m (172,160 sq ft). On entering the building, the impressive view is of ever more, larger, rooms, opening up. There are nine doorways leading to the main nave. The church's turbulent history is made evident by the adjoining works of Islamic and Byzantine art. Not to be missed in the left (northern)

aisle is the "sweating column", its secret having since been revealed, however – the column draws the moisture from a cistern lying beneath it. The two emperors Justinian the Great and Constantine the Great are depicted in a magnificent mosaic in the Hagia Sophia's outer atrium.

It was Constantine the Great who reunited the Roman Empire, making Byzantion the capital that was renamed Constantinople in his memory. It is also from him that the name "Hagia Sophia" (Holy Wisdom) comes, the name already given to the building preceding the present-day church. Its foundation stone was laid by Emperor Justinian the Great who later proclaimed: "the church thus became magnificent beyond all measure …"

Constantine (c. 280–337) was born in Naissus, present-day Niš in Serbia, as the son of the head of the military and later Emperor Constantius Chlorus and his concubine, later canonized as Saint Helena. At the age of just 13 he was taken to the Roman imperial court in Nicomedia, now Izmir, as a hostage to ensure the imperial equilibrium under the three Roman rulers of the day. In 305 he fled to his father who was slain in 306 in a battle against the Picts in Eboracum – now the city of York in England. Constantine had himself appointed emperor by his father's troops and, together with Severus II, became the joint ruler of the west of the Roman Empire, residing in Gaul. Autocracy was something he still had to fight for, however. The decisive turn of events, also for the promotion of the Christian legend, was the battle on the Milvian Bridge near Rome in 312, when Constantine defeated

the West Roman Emperor Maxentius "in the name of the Cross". Twelve years later, in 324, he achieved his goal: Constantine was ruler of the Roman world and introduced the dynastic principle of hereditary succession to the throne. He proclaimed Constantinople as the imperial capital.

A 10th-century mosaic in the southern vestibule of the Hagia Sophia depicts Mary with child (left). She is seated on a throne between the Emperors Justinian the Great and Constantine the Great. Justinian, to her right, presents Mary with a church, the Hagia Sophia; Constantine, on her left, hands her a city: Constantinople. Above: Constantine as depicted in a fresco from the 11th century in the Elmali Kilise (Apple Church) in Göreme.

THIS SIDE OF THE GOLDEN HORN:
THE OLD TOWN AND EYÜP

Ahmed I (c. 1589–1617), the first Sultan of the Ottoman Empire, who ascended the throne as a minor (1603), wanted to create a monument to himself with the construction of a mosque bearing his name. It was to be larger and lovelier than the nearby Hagia Sophia and – as an expression of especially lofty ambitions – it was to have golden minarets. The sultan selected the southeast side of the Hippodrome as the site, commissioning the court architect Mehmet Tahir Ağa (c. 1540–1617), a student of Sinan (c. 1490–1588), the most important architect of his time, with its construction. The

To detract from the sacrilege of the Sultan Ahmed Mosque having six minarets (above right) – a number reserved for the Al Hasram Mosque in Mecca – the young ruler is said to have donated a seventh minaret for Mecca. He was not able to enjoy the sight of his own mosque (above: one of the passageways, right: the atrium with the old washing fountains) for long, however, as he died in the year following its completion.

SULTAN AHMED MOSQUE
(BLUE MOSQUE)

mosque was built between 1609 and 1616, however, golden minarets would have exceeded the budget, and this is why Ahmed's architect is said to have "misheard" the Turkish number "altı" (six) instead of "altın" (golden). He built two more minarets than was usual practice – out of stone.

THIS SIDE OF THE GOLDEN HORN:
THE OLD TOWN AND EYÜP

It is no accident that the Sultan Ahmed Mosque is also known as the Blue Mosque. More than 21,000 blue-green ceramic tiles from Iznik, famous for its tile production since the mid-15th century, were used for its cladding. Stylized images of lilies, carnations, tulips and roses decorate the tiles, which are resplendent in the subdued light of the more than 250 windows in the mosque. The main load of the dome is supported by four fluted columns, a good 5 m (16 ft) in diameter and often referred to as the "elephant feet". The design of the mosque's prayer pulpit (the minbar), installed by Sultan

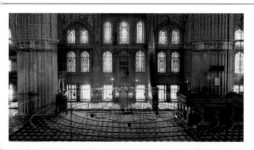

Murat III, was based on that on that in Mecca and, like the prayer niches (the mihrab), it is made of white marble. The latter are adorned with precious stones, also said to include a fragment from the Kaaba in Mecca. At night the Blue Mosque is beautifully illuminated by colored floodlights.

The Sultan Ahmed Mosque has been Istanbul's main mosque since the secularization of the Hagia Sophia. Entry is strictly prohibited to non-Muslims during prayer times. The dimensions of the mosque's 53 x 51 m (174 x 167 ft) interior are overwhelming. With a diameter of 23.5 m (77 ft), the main dome has a crown height of 43 m (141 ft). Its weight is borne by a further four half domes, each supported in turn by three conches.

THIS SIDE OF THE GOLDEN HORN: THE OLD TOWN AND EYÜP

It does not matter whether you sip the first coffee of the day here in the morning or stroll past the around 40 shops in the evening, the atmosphere at the Arasta Bazaar always tends to be peaceful and tranquil, unlike the permanently overcrowded Grand Bazaar. It was originally the site of stables built in the 17th century at the same time as the nearby Sultan Ahmed Mosque and which once formed part of the mosque complex. The historic wooden constructions were destroyed by a series of fires but the former stables were restored in the 1980s and converted into shops. Today jewel-

The market halls of the Arasta Bazaar, where carpets and leather bags are also sold next to the various artisan and craft works, shelter in the shadow of the nearby Sultan Ahmed Mosque. As the bazaar is one of the less crowded you can observe the less hectic activity here in peace and quiet, perhaps even enjoying a cup of tea. The bazaar also has a passageway leading to the Mosaic Museum.

ry, spices, textiles and a wide variety of arts and crafts are on offer at the bazaar every day. The earnings from the shop rentals are used for the maintenance of the Sultan Ahmed Mosque. Some of Istanbul's best-known carpet and ceramics dealers are to be found in the surrounding streets.

THIS SIDE OF THE GOLDEN HORN:
THE OLD TOWN AND EYÜP

Ever since Constantine the Great made Byzantion the capital of the Roman Empire, the grounds of the Great Palace of the Byzantine emperors (according to historic sources, a complex comprising several palace buildings and pavilions surrounded by gardens) extended over a huge hill area at a height of 31 m (102 ft) in six terraces from the Hippodrome as far as the Hagia Sophia and then down to the Sea of Marmara. It was only in the 13th century that these buildings began to fall into decay, with apartment buildings later being built on the site. In the 1930s and 1950s, magnificent mosaic

floors once belonging to the peristyle, the colonnade-lined courtyards of Byzantine palace complexes, were discovered to the south-east of the Sultan Ahmed Mosque. A cohesive area of antique mosaic flooring, measuring about 250 sq m (2,690 ft) in size, is on display in the Mosaic Museum.

Many of the Great Palace's secrets still lie buried at a depth of up to 8 m (26 ft) below today's street level but some walls have been left visible (above), still providing an impression of their former magnificence. The mosaics, produced in the 5th and 6th centuries under Emperor Justinian the Great, were once Antiquity's most comprehensive natural history mosaic and were painstakingly restored during 14 years of precision work.

Istanbul was largely still a "wooden city" until well into the 20th century. Almost all of the traditional houses on the Bosphorus were built in a similar manner, with Istanbul's town houses featuring a stone-built ground floor and one or two upper floors made of wood. In these houses there was no need for peeping from behind the curtains because, when curiosity got the better of them, the female residents could look out through the wooden frames of the upper floor windows without being seen themselves. Ravaged by a series of fires in the city, these historic constructions came to be replaced with more solid structures and materials instead of rebuilding with wood. The largest cohesive wooden house district in Istanbul was still in existence along the Atatürk Bulvarı in the Zeyrek quarter until well into the 1970s, but traditional wooden buildings eventually came

ISTANBUL'S TRADITIONAL WOODEN HOUSES AND THE RAVAGES OF TIME

under threat throughout the city. Efforts are being made to preserve some of the old buildings, the houses are also under threat from developers and lack of woodworking skills. Many have since fallen into disrepair, their broken panes no longer providing the occasion for discrete peeping.

Traditional wooden houses (left and above: near the Süleymaniye Mosque) are still to be seen in some parts of Istanbul, albeit in a wretched state at times. The Soğukçeşme Sokağı, a cobblestone alleyway near Gülhane Park, is testimony to the successful renovation of the pastel houses. There are also a number of lovely examples in the Sultan Ahmed District around the mosque of the same name.

THIS SIDE OF THE GOLDEN HORN:
THE OLD TOWN AND EYÜP

One of the most important historical settings in Istanbul, the Hippodrome, has lost much of its former grandeur. Its design is reminiscent of the Circus Maximus in Rome, building work having begun in 203 under the Roman Emperor Septimius Severus and then extended under Constantine the Great in the 4th century as a magnificently decorated arena for horse and chariot racing – The gigantic (around 480 m/ 1,575 ft long and 120 m/394 ft wide) ellipse-shaped, two-floored grandstands accommodated audiences of more than 10,0000 spectators, and the founding ceremony for the

"new Rome" was held here on 11 May 330, The stands were however completely destroyed and plundered during the Fourth Crusade (1202 to 1204). The famous four bronze horses, for instance, which are now on display in Venice, once adorned a quadriga at the Hippodrome in Constantinople.

The best-preserved testimony to the ancient Hippodrome is the almost 20-m-high (66-ft) Egyptian Obelisk (above), erected by Pharaoh Thutmose III in Karnak in the 15th century BC and brought to Istanbul by Emperor Theodosius I in 390. Four carved reliefs on the marble base depict Theodosius and his family in a box at the Hippodrome (left). Top: The "German Fountain" on the north-east perimeter, donated by Emperor Wilhelm II in 1898.

Sokollu Mehmet Pasha (1505 to 1579) was a member of an aristocratic Bosnian family from Sokoloviç and was brought to the city on the Bosphorus as part of the devshirme system, practiced during the Ottoman Empire on the Balkan Peninsula in particular. This system was a means of forcibly recruiting young Christian boys, which then had to convert to Islam and were to be trained as Janissaries. In Istanbul Pasha gained the trust of Sultan Suleiman I and ultimately became the Grand Vizier to three sultans. The small mosque with just one minaret named after him and

donated by his wife Esmahan Sultan, daughter of Selim II, is situated on a steep slope to the south-west of the Hippodrome. It was built between 1571 and 1572 on the site of a Byzantine church. It is considered to be an accomplished late work by the legendary Ottoman architect Sinan.

This mosque owes one of its special features to its confined location. Unlike in other mosques, the madrasah, the theological college, was not designed as a separate building but integrated into the atrium of the mosque. Some of the magnificent tiles in the interior are still the originals from the 16th century. The prayer pulpit is said to feature two black stones from the Kaaba in Mecca.

Formerly known as the Church of the Saints Sergius and Bacchus and then converted to a mosque at the beginning of the 16th century under Beyazıt II (c. 1447–1512), the "Little Hagia Sophia" is located somewhere not far from the Sokollu Mehmet Pasha Mosque heading south toward the Sea of Marmara. Built a few years prior to its "big sister", shortly after its benefactor Emperor Justinian the Great came to power in 527 and completed by 536, the church dedicated is to two early Christian martyrs and once formed part of the Great Palace of the Byzantine emperors. Rather modest in its

KÜÇÜK AYASOFYA MOSQUE
(THE LITTLE HAGIA SOPHIA) 11

external appearance, its special feature is its geometric construction incorporating a central octagonal domed area in an irregular rectangle. Inside there is a beautiful two-level colonnade on three sides. Later additions as a mosque included an atrium with washing fountains and a minaret.

Like the Hagia Sophia, the interior of its "little sister" was also originally decorated with gold mosaics. Last renovated in 2007, the mosque is now beautifully whitewashed. The Islamic features facing toward Mecca, namely the prayer niches (mihrab) and pulpit (minbar), are positioned diagonally to the axis of the interior dominated by a 20-m-high (66–ft) dome supported by eight columns.

It quickly becomes clear why Istanbul's largest, ancient preserved cistern is also called Yerebatan Sarayı, or "Sunken Palace", when one descends the steps and sets off along the boardwalk to explore the fascinating underworld said to have been created as early as the 4th century under Constantine the Great. The version we see today, however, was not achieved until extension work began in 532 under Emperor Justinian I. Since then, it has measured 140 m (459 ft) in length and just under 70 m (230 ft) in width, with a volumetric capacity of around 80,000 cu m (2,825,173 cu ft). A total of 336 well-preserved

columns, measuring up to 8 m (26 ft) high and arranged in twelve rows, support the brick vault and create a reflection in the dark water. It is pleasantly cool down here, even in summer. A tape recording plays classical music, water trickles away quietly, and floodlights give the scene a magical aura.

"Cisterna Basilica" was the name given to the cistern filled by the sources further up the Bosphorus River during the time of Emperor Justinian I – a name relating to a church built above it, but which has not been preserved. Part of a larger system, it was the water supply for the Great Palace. The two Medusa heads in the northwest corner are famous, and probably once denoted a sanctuary of water nymphs, before being "recycled" here as pedestals.

THIS SIDE OF THE GOLDEN HORN:
THE OLD TOWN AND EYÜP

The staff at the Cağaloğlu Hamam, one of the city's finest historic bathhouses, love to take time out to patiently demonstrate to visitors (many of whom are foreigners) the traditional procedure of lathering, massaging, sweating and resting. The bathhouse, located just a few minutes' walk north-west of the entrance to the Yerebatan Cistern, was built in 1741 by order of Sultan Mahmud I. There are separate entrances for men and women, and both sections have identical designs: guests enter the bath via the reception room (camekan), where they are provided with hand towels and

At the center of the room in the Cağaloğlu Hamam is a giant marble slab on which one can receive a professional massage from head to toe – an experience which Mark Twain did not deem to be overly pleasant: "Presently my man sat me down by a tank of hot water, drenched me well, gloved his hand with a coarse mitten, and began to polish me all over with it."

soap, and can relax over a cup of tea after the bath. The warm room (soğuluk) leads into the actual steam bath (hararet) – the center of every Turkish bath, where you can stay as long as you like. Visitors have included Franz Liszt, Florence Nightingale, Tony Curtis and Jenson Button among others.

The baroque façade of the Nuruosmaniye Mosque is a striking contrast to its plain, modest interior. Construction began as early as 1748 under Mahmud I, but was not completed until 1755 during the reign of Osman III (1699–1757), who succeeded his brother Mahmud on the throne and after whom the mosque was named, the Turkish "nuruosmaniye" meaning "Light of Osman". The inside of the dome bears a quotation (Çyat an-nur) from the 35th verse of the 24th Sura of the Koran, describing God as the light of the heavens and earth – which may be an indication of the

The Nuruosmaniye Mosque marks the south-eastern way into the Grand Bazaar (right: looking out over the domes of the bazaar toward the mosque; top right: an overall view of the structure whose exterior features baroque style elements). Those wanting to avoid the hustle and bustle of the bazaar will find contemplative silence and tranquility inside the mosque, where daylight pours in through five rows of tall windows (above).

Sultan's desire to be God'
equal. The architecture of the
single-domed mosque, which
sits atop a deep basement, displays the first examples of
Ottoman baroque styles. The
mosque's forecourt, laid out in
a horseshoe-shape for space
reasons, was an architectural
innovation of the time.

THIS SIDE OF THE GOLDEN HORN: THE OLD TOWN AND EYÜP

Anyone who mentions the word "bazaar" in Istanbul is primarily referring to the Kapalı Çarşi, the Grand (or literally "covered") Bazaar. The world's largest Oriental market is a city in itself, "a monstrous hive of little shops" (so said Mark Twain), and a tourist attraction which locals, such as the Istanbul-born Nobel Literature Prize winner Orhan Pamuk (born in 1952), "prefer to avoid", although it is a must for everyone else. The bazaar is surrounded by a high wall with twenty-two gates, and sprawls over an area of more than 300,000 sq m (3,228,000 sq ft) between the Nuruosmaniye

Mosque in the east and the Beyazit Mosque in the west. The goings on in its sixty-one darkened, largely covered streets and corridors are incredibly vibrant and diverse. Here, in the mercantile heart of the city, some 4,400 stores and almost 2,200 workshops await custom with a great array of wares.

The respective corridors are traditionally reserved for specific groups of items; cafés and restaurants provide refreshments, while mosques cater to spiritual wellbeing. The bazaar originated from an initial, modest market hall built under Mehmet II (Fatih) in 1461, which was gradually replaced by a hall of pillars spanned by fifteen domes. More and more merchants and craftsmen clustered around these over time.

The selection is almost endless: the Grand Bazaar is not the only place where rug shops line up one after another and merchants peddle their vivid wares. The old art of carpet-weaving has a long tradition in Turkey and has been passed down from generation to generation. The merchants love to extend a harmless invitation into their shops over a cup of tea, based on the motto that "looking is free". This is when they chat about the various products they offer. There are generally two types of carpets: knotted and woven. Knotted rugs are used as dowries; they hang decoratively on walls or lie on the floor to generate warmth. The tightness and the density of the knots is crucial in determining the quality and the value of the rug. In genuine hand-knotted rugs, this is easy to see, and the pile cannot be pulled out. The rugs are made using pure, usually live, wool, or sometimes even silk, while

mixtures of cotton or synthetic materials tend to lower the cost. Woven carpets *(kilims)* are smaller. They may be purely decorative, but are often used as prayer mats and have a "prayer pattern" depicting, for example, the relief of a *mihrab* (prayer niche) or the tree of life as a symbol of immortality.

"If you want to know a person, do business with him" is a phrase said to have been uttered by Muhammad, the prophet and founder of Islam, who himself probably participated in trade journeys. And a rug shop provides ample opportunity to do this (all pictures: in the Grand Bazaar) and to haggle *(pazarlık)*, although the latter does require some time – it is considered uncouth to talk about the prices straight away.

THIS SIDE OF THE GOLDEN HORN:
THE OLD TOWN AND EYÜP

Istanbul was famous as the "city of books" as early as the 16th century: a Moroccan messenger who visited Istanbul in 1589–90 reported of "books in vast quantities" and is said to have wanted to "take home quite a large number of extremely interesting [books]". It is well possible that he struck gold at the Book Bazaar: he would only have had to walk through a vine-covered gate a short distance south-west of the Grand Bazaar and descend into the narrow alleyway of the Book Bazaar (Sahaflar Çarşısı), where new and ancient books, from Turkey and from foreign countries, historic engravings,

calendar pages and printed posters are sold. Further west, the lane opens out onto a small square, where a monument pays tribute to Ibrahim Müteferrika, a scholar, publisher and printer of Hungarian origin, who opened the Ottoman Empire's first print shop with Arabic type in Istanbul in 1726.

Although most items sold at the Book Bazaar are in Turkish, it is also possible to find specialized international literature, travel guides, language guides, calligraphy and miniatures. Those who spend some time here can make some real discoveries. The first book published by Ibrahim Müteferrika (who is honored at the bazaar) at his print shop incidentally appeared in 1729 and was a Turkish-Arabic dictionary.

In Turkey, everyone loves gold. Whether it be for the New Year, a birthday or a wedding, there is always some reason to give gold jewelry to a loved one. And the goldsmiths here have a millennia-old tradition: gold was processed into jewelry in Anatolia as early as the 3rd millennium BC. Unlike with carpets, haggling is not advisable, indeed fruitless, when you are intending to buy goldware – gold jewelry is sold by weight, and the daily price is definitive. This price is advertised on a sign hung up in the shop windows, in front of which the potential customers, tirelessly staring at the goods on display, stand and talk shop about the finest pieces with the air of experts. Chains, earrings, bracelets, rings, coins, bars are sold in their thousands in the shops and then hoarded away in beautifully worked treasure chests, locked cupboard drawers and safes by their happy and proud new owners.

Gold jewelry is so coveted in Turkey that private households are estimated to hold some 5,000 tons of the precious metal. Istanbul's Grand Bazaar in (all pictures) alone has more than 1,000 jewelers, and there are said to be around 35,000 throughout the country. The valuable commodity is also sought after abroad: local goldsmiths made their country the second-largest exporter of gold jewelry items after Italy.

TRADITIONAL HANDICRAFTS: GOLD AND SILVER JEWELRY

Silver jewelry is also very coveted. Traditional patterns are worked into 800- to 900-carat silver by hand. Anatolian folk jewelry, book jackets, mirrors, cutlery and jewel cases are all made this way, and even some silver earrings, bracelets and belts are recrafted by artisans based on the originals.

THIS SIDE OF THE GOLDEN HORN:
THE OLD TOWN AND EYÜP

According to the inscriptions above the main entrance and in the courtyard, Sultan Beyazit II (c. 1447–1512), son of Mehmet II (Fatih), had the mosque bearing his name erected during the first decade of the 16th century, making it the city's oldest preserved sultan's mosque. He allegedly entrusted the task of designing and constructing the building to Yakub Şah Bin Sultan Şah, who created the perfect example of classic Ottoman architecture, which also incorporates elements from the Hagia Sophia and the Green Mosque in Bursa. The mosque's garden was once home to a soup kitchen, which

was converted into a library in 1880. The mosque itself rises up on the east of the Beyazit Meydanı, one of the liveliest squares in the Old Town. The former madrasah on the western side houses a calligraphy museum, with old Koran manuscripts, as well as Tuğras – calligraphic Sultan signatures.

The mighty main dome of the Beyazit Mosque rests on four solid marble pillars and two porphyry columns. Supported by two larger semi-domes on the longitudinal axis, above the entrance and above the *mihrab* (prayer niche), it is reminiscent of the Hagia Sophia complex. Four smaller domes line both the north-eastern and south-western side of the mosque.

THIS SIDE OF THE GOLDEN HORN:
THE OLD TOWN AND EYÜP

Visible from afar, the mosque of Sultan Süleyman I is perched majestically atop the third of the Old Town's hills, above the Golden Horn. Its lofty location also an expression of the self-confidence of its founder, who was experiencing the peak of his power at the time of its construction, between 1550 and 1557. But the master builder Sinan, acclaimed as the "Poet of Stones" as well as the "Ottoman Michelangelo", also used this building to create a monument to himself: in order to meet the strict requirements of his client, who had asked for the mosque to "stay standing for as long as the world exists",

SÜLEYMANIYE MOSQUE

Sinan built the structure on a foundation considered to be earthquake-proof. The main dome of the mosque is today the second-largest in Istanbul after that of the Hagia Sophia, and the giant mosque complex as a whole is the city's largest comparable ensemble and one of its best-known sites.

The mosque's four minarets, along with their ten balconies, represent the fact that Süleyman I was the fourth sultan since the capture of the city, and the tenth ruler of the Ottoman Empire. Surrounding the central, walled area of the mosque is a giant complex housing social and charity facilities, stretching down over several terraces as far as the Golden Horn.

THIS SIDE OF THE GOLDEN HORN:
THE OLD TOWN AND EYÜP

The mosque's interior is bright and spacious: light floods in through the 138 windows, while vivid tiles from Iznik make for fine decorations. The overwhelmingly beautiful main dome, measuring 54 m (177 ft) high and 27.5 m (90 ft) in diameter, rests on four solid pillars and comprises two shells between which Sinan inserted sixty-four rounded clay cylinders. Their openings look into the approximately 58 by 57-m-large (190 by 187-ft) prayer room, thus creating excellent acoustics. The former imperial box of the Byzantine hippodrome was "looted" in order to adorn the mosque's interior

For some one thousand years, Byzantine and Ottoman master-builders had tried to surpass, or at least equal, the Hagia Sophia in terms of aesthetic grace and monumental magnificence. But it was not until Mimar Sinan, who was appointed the court's chief architect and civil engineer by Süleyman I in 1538, that the challenge of almost weight-lessly placing a similarly sized dome on top a giant, light-filled room was eventually met.

SÜLEYMANIYE MOSQUE

courtyard with columns made of pink granite and white marble. More than 3,000 workers and craftsmen were involved with the construction, which the master-builder Sinan "only" considered to be his "journeyman's piece" – he regarded the Selimiye Mosque in Edirne as his masterpiece.

The Rüstem Paşa Mosque, erected in just two years between 1561 and 1563 for the grand vizier of the same name, is yet another example of Sinan's unparalleled architectural mastery. There was no denying the fact that his client, a native of Sarajevo who was also the son-in-law of Süley-man I, possessed a certain degree of business acumen, and this probably also played a major role in choosing the location of his mosque – in the middle of the lively, crowded commercial district of Tah-takale, situated on the Golden Horn, the architect virtually had to place the structure on a

"pedestal", that is on a solid substructure, which would raise it high above the everyday hustle and bustle; but this substructure also had the advantage of being able to house various stores, workshops and warehouses, whose rent practically covered the costs for maintaining the mosque.

The Rüstem Paşa Mosque is famous for its almost completely preserved faïence adornments. The forecourt itself contains a spectacular display of tiles, while in the mosque's interior, the cool ceramics from Iznik and Kütahya stretch as far as the uppermost section of windows (above and top). Also worth seeing are the marble features and the pulpit which is decorated with mother-of-pearl marquetry (left) – a masterpiece of woodwork.

The Egyptian Bazaar, originally built as a caravansary under architect Kasım Ağa around 1660, and which was considered a safe haven for merchants to store their goods, attend to their business and spend the night, was part of the Yeni Mosque complex even in the early days. When, in the following century, the caravan heyday gradually diminished because goods were increasingly being transported on real ships as opposed to "ships of the desert", the caravansary was transformed into a bazaar named the Egyptian Bazaar or Mısır Çarşısı, since many of the goods had once been imported

from Egypt. For a time known as the New Bazaar, there is no need to explain why the L-shaped indoor market is also known as the "Spice Bazaar" – just let your nose guide you on that one! In addition to all sorts of spices, you can also find dried fruits, nuts, seeds and Turkish delights here.

Visitors to the Egyptian Bazaar, located near the Yeni Mosque, are instantly hit with the wafting fragrances and aromas of the Orient. On both sides of the covered street, some 100 merchants provide a feast for the senses with an array of colors, shapes and smells. Nowhere else in Istanbul are so many spices – whether cumin or pepper, paprika or saffron, vanilla or cinnamon – all presented as attractively as they are here.

THIS SIDE OF THE GOLDEN HORN:
THE OLD TOWN AND EYÜP

Unlike most of the city's large mosques, the Yeni does not sit in an exposed location perched on a hill, but is instead situated near the southern end of the Galata Bridge on the Golden Horn. A lady, Safiye Sultan, the mother of Mehmet III (1566–1603), was the driving force behind its construction, which began in 1597– she pulled the strings in the harem from 1595, when her son ascended the throne. However, the sultan's death saw the work on the "New Mosque" ("Yeni Camii") slow down, and a fire in 1660 destroyed the half-finished building. The present look of the mosque, completed in 1663

The royal architect, Mustafa Ağa, commissioned by Hatice Turhan Sultan, designed the mosque's interior and exterior in a "classical" style: staggered side domes and two minarets are adjoined to the 36-m-high (118-ft) main dome in cascades (above); the interior is adorned with faïence ceramics from Iznik. Top right: This small palace, Hünkar Kasrı, gave the ruler access to the sultan's lodge, which can only be visited from the outside.

after just three years, is also attributed to a woman: Hatice Turhan Sultan, the mother of Mehmet IV (1642–1693). A covered passageway leads from the sultan's lodge in the prayer house to a small palace, Hünkar Kasrı, which has been re-opened to the public since 2010 following restorations.

THIS SIDE OF THE GOLDEN HORN:
THE OLD TOWN AND EYÜP

The horn signals from the ships and ferries in the harbor of Eminönü can be heard from as far as the Egyptian Bazaar. This place is like a beehive – Istanbul locals on their way to another part of the city, tourists off on a daytrip, interspersed with beverage and snack vendors peddling their various goods. Exploring the city and its surrounds from the water is a great way to gain new insights and perspectives – whether this be by jumping over the Golden Horn to Beyoğlu, traveling on to Üsküdar on the Asian side, or cruising the Bosphorus as far as the fishing village of Rumeli Kavagi

"Eminönü" was also the name of the Istanbul district which was independent until 2008 and which is now classified as part of the Fatih district, originally its western neighbor. Located at the tip of the Old Town peninsula at the southern end of the Galata Bridge, and today one of the biggest traffic hubs on the European side of Istanbul, it is here that the oldest settlement in ancient Byzantium was founded.

on the European side or to Anadolu Kavaği on the Asian side, the terminus of the city's steamboat. The Port of Eminönü has six piers, where the motor launches are moored alongside the ferries and water buses – high-speed catamarans which also call in at the Princes' Islands in summer.

THIS SIDE OF THE GOLDEN HORN:
THE OLD TOWN AND EYÜP

Those setting foot on the Galata Bridge for the first time may get the impression that this is the heart and soul of Istanbul. Fishermen stand on top, while bright cushions wait to be sat on by as many guests as possible, both inside and outside the cafés and restaurants, and vendors selling sesame bread rings scurry about – they are all busy, but there is always time for a quick chat. The roar of the traffic is as incessant as the photographs of the city skyline taken by travelers on either side of the Golden Horn. Following two wooden constructions, an iron bridge spanned the river between the Old Town

and New Town, Eminönü and Karaköy, for the first time in 1875. This was replaced by a two-level pontoon bridge in 1912. The present-day bridge, completed in 1992 and measuring 42 m (138 ft) wide, is also a two-level construction designed by German engineer, Fritz Leonhart (1909–1999).

Supported by 114 pylons, today's Galata Bridge is the first bridge across the Golden Horn to be firmly fixed into the subgrade. For years, the commercial areas beneath the roadway lay empty, but have been home to many cafés and restaurants since 2002 (left: looking back at the Yeni Mosque in Eminönü; top: view of the Galata Bridge in Karaköy). Above: Despite the eight lanes available for traffic, the bridge is often a clogged bottleneck.

The myths and legends surrounding the Golden Horn are like one of the tales out of *One Thousand and One Nights*. The earlier rulers are said to have decorated their palaces with so much gold that their brilliance rivaled that of the sun and served as an inspiration for naming the bay which branches off westward from the Bosphorus and divides the European part of the city. Another story recounts that, when the Ottomans moved in, the Byzantines threw their (gold) treasures into the port basin, giving the water a golden shimmer and the bay its name. Modern-day Istanbul has a much more prosaic view of the matter. There, the Golden Horn is simply known as "Haliç" (bay, gulf). In actual fact, the bay is a river valley which became submerged toward the end of the last Ice Age; but the myths and legends surrounding the Golden Horn are much more exciting attempts at explaining the ori-

gins of the inlet. One story says, for example, that its entrance was once protected by a large chain, but that Sultan Mehmet II, who was not called Fatih ("the conqueror") for nothing, overcame this barrier by quickly hauling his ships onto the land before setting them back into the water.

Orhan Pamuk recalls a steamboat ride on the Golden Horn: "The coexistence of great history and oppressive poverty, of openness to external influences and a wonderfully preserved community spirit, of ostentatious natural and artistic beauty and an everyday life patched up from shaky, precarious relationships – does Istanbul's secret lie somewhere in there?"

THIS SIDE OF THE GOLDEN HORN:
THE OLD TOWN AND EYÜP

The advertising sign "Whirling Dervishes – men and women together" reveals that the magnificent Sirkeci train station now regularly hosts performances by the whirling dervishes. Who would have thought? Here, at this historic place, which Sultan Abdul-Hamid II had built near the confluence of the Golden Horn and the Bosphorus in 1890 in order to create a stylish setting for diplomats, spies, adventurers, conmen and kings traveling on the Orient Express? These glorious days are long gone, the present-day main entrance to the train station is now housed in a plain, modern outbuilding,

and it is now the Turkish national rail (TCDD) in operation rather than the legendary train of old. But under the high ceilings of the historic station, designed by the Berlin architect August Jachmund in a mix of Art Nouveau and "Orientalized" elements, the whirling dervishes, at least, still dance.

Dervishes can today be found spinning around at the place where the legendary Orient Express trains once drew in. The white, bell-shaped skirts of the dancers, whose twirling movements send them into an ecstatic trance bringing them closer to God, are striking. They hold their right hand palm-up to receive God's blessing, while the downward facing left hand transfers the blessing to the earth.

THIS SIDE OF THE GOLDEN HORN:
THE OLD TOWN AND EYÜP

Sultan Süleyman II very likely had the "Prince's Mosque" built in memory of his son Mehmet, who died of a smallpox infection in 1543 at the age of twenty-two. Sinan, who had previously only excelled in building bridges and fortresses and who had no experience in large places of worship, was commissioned with this task. In his own words, this job was his "apprentice piece" — and yet it displays the full mastery of this exceptionally talented architect. For this mosque too, erected between 1545 and 1548 on a square ground plan, master-builder Sinan drew his inspirations from the Byzantine

cross-in-square church structures. The mausoleums of Prince
Mehmet and Grand Viziers
Ibrahim Paşa and Rüstem Paşa
at the rear of the mosque are
works of art in themselves. The
türbe (tomb) of Prince Mehmet,
the sultan's favorite son who
died when still young, is undoubtedly the most attractive.

Mighty columns support the
mosque's approximately 37-m-
high (121-ft) (diameter: 18 m/59
ft) main dome, which Sinan combined with four (instead of two)
smaller half-domes, each in turn
with two smaller half-shells, for
the first time. The exterior of this
permanent memento is adorned
with cascading domed roofs and
two slender, grooved minarets.

THIS SIDE OF THE GOLDEN HORN:
THE OLD TOWN AND EYÜP

The city was supplied with water by this originally 1,000-m-long (3,281-ft) aqueduct for some 1,500 years, until the late 19th century. The water came from sources up the Bosphorus River in the Belgrade Forest, situated about 30 km (19 miles) to the north, and was then channeled into a giant cistern, which acted as a central water distributor at the present-day Bayzıt Square.

Constantine the Great had already been involved with his new capital's water supply, before Flavius Valens (328–378, Roman emperor from 364) completed an elaborate system of underground pipes, tunnels,

canals and cisterns. As part of this system, the aqueduct, named after the emperor and built in 375, spans the valley between the third and fourth hill of the Old Town. Later extensively renovated, more than two-thirds of the structure, built from roughly hewn blocks, have been preserved today.

Modernity meets antiquity: the water was channeled down two canals with a gradient of 1:1000 to the two-level aqueduct, whose arches are between 18 and 26 m (59 and 85 ft) high. Today, the grand ten-lane Ataturk Bulvarı road takes the traffic right through the ancient archways.

THIS SIDE OF THE GOLDEN HORN:
THE OLD TOWN AND EYÜP

The city's fourth hill was once home to the Church of the Holy Apostles consecrated as early as the 4th century during the time of Constantine the Great, and renovated under Emperor Justinian I in the 6th century – it was the second most important church in the city and Ottoman Empire after Hagia Sophia, and a burial place for Byzantine emperors until the 11th century. Nothing remains of this church, whose structure was probably used as a model for the famous Basilica di San Marco in Venice. The precious remains of the Apostle St Andrew and his students St Luke and St Timothy were stolen

FETHIYE MOSQUE
(PAMMAKARISTOS CHURCH)

church of St George does today. Only after this time, in
1591, Murat III (1546–1595)
converted the church to a
mosque wishing to display his
gratitude for his recent victo-
ries. It is for this reason that
the mosque was also given the
name of Fethiye Camii ("Conqueror's Mosque").

THIS SIDE OF THE GOLDEN HORN:
THE OLD TOWN AND EYÜP

For centuries, the Old Town continued to spread further westward, and the newly created districts became home to two larger ethnic groups – the Greeks in Phanar (Fener) and the Jews in Balat. City fortifications were successively built to protect the borders of the ever-expanding city, and the Chora church is an example of this – it was erected between 527 and 575 outside the city walls originally built under Emperor Constantine, on the slopes of the city's sixth hill. The church was thus originally located out on the open "terrain" or "land" (Greek: *chora*), which also explains its name, and was later

The building situated near the Theodosian city wall was erected in the late 11th century, and constantly modified in the centuries which followed (top right). The stunning mosaics depicting the Virgin Mary and the Life of Christ (above) date back to the early 14th century. The frescoes, most likely created by the same unknown masters, are less famous but just as imposing (right).

surrounded by the new wall built by Emperor Theodosius. Like most Byzantine places of worship, it too was converted into a mosque in 1511 by the Ottoman rulers and the images were plastered over. Restored after 1948, it is today a public museum featuring some fine mosaics and frescoes inside.

THIS SIDE OF THE GOLDEN HORN: THE OLD TOWN AND EYÜP

The city fortifications, built under, and named after, Emperor Theodosius II (401–450), were to remain a bastion of the Christian Occident for more than a thousand years. Building the wall became necessary due to the prospering city's dramatic growth – shifting the border westward more than doubled the urban area suitable for building – and due to the migration of peoples, which resulted in Constantinople coming under an intense threat from the Goths and the Huns. To ensure protection was not just limited to land, Theodosius II also ordered the construction of sea fortifications at

With its eleven gates, 20-m-wide (66-ft) moat and 192 approximately 20-m-tall (66-ft) towers, the almost 7-km-long (4-mile) double line of walls, made from red bricks and hewn limestone blocks, and situated between the Sea of Marmara and the Golden Horn, was considered impenetrable (right, top right: the ruins of the Tekfur Palace). Mehmet II (Fatih) incidentally had it repaired after the conquest of Constantinople.

the Golden Horn and the Sea of Marmara in the year 439, meaning the city was now also fully enclosed by a fortress. This structure was able to withstand even earthquakes in the centuries which followed, but not the attack by Mehmet II (Fatih) and his troops, who conquered the city in 1453.

THIS SIDE OF THE GOLDEN HORN:
THE OLD TOWN AND EYÜP

When Abu Ayyub (Turkish: "Eyüp") al-Ansari fell during the first Arab siege of Constantinople (674–678) launched under his supreme command, he was already a very old man who – as a comrade and as a standard-bearer for the Prophet Muhammad – had lived an eventful life. An anonymously composed chronicle states that "As he knew he would die, he issued the following order: 'Bare your swords and attack the fortress. Wherever you are able to go, bury me there during the war and make my grave unrecognizable'". And that is what happened, although the grave did not

remain hidden for long after the Muslims retreated, and quickly became a pilgrimage site which continues to attract Muslim pilgrims from all over the world even today. After Mehmet II (Fatih) conquered Constantinople in 1453, a dignified tomb and mosque was built there for Eyüp instead.

Eyüp's tomb (left), in front of which Muslim pilgrims pray to Allah to this day, was incorporated into the forecourt of the mosque originally erected in 1458. When this had fallen victim to an earthquake in the 18th century, the complex was completely rebuilt. The Ottoman princes were traditionally girt with the sword of the dynasty's founder, Osman, in front of the tomb before actually being enthroned at the Topkapı Palace.

"Tate alla turca" filled the headlines in 2006 when, to mark Istanbul's appointment as Europe's capital of culture for 2010, a mammoth new international art project was presented. It had been developed at the initiative of Bilgi University (founded in 1994) and largely financed by private investors. Modeled on London's Tate Modern art gallery, the atmospheric setting is that of an imposing industrial ruin – the first electricity plant in the Ottoman Empire, which was erected in an industrial district on the Golden Horn and which supplied the city with power for seventy years from 1911

If "the" Tate Modern (in London) is the focus of classical modernity, this "Tate" (alla Turca) could well become the art haven of Eastern Europe. Opened in 2007, its approximately 118,000-sq-m (1,269,680-sq-ft) area is now an international platform for art, culture and the sciences – a creative quarter with a vast space for exhibits, events, lectures and workshops, as well as an energy and design museum.

until the closure of the plant in 1983. The name is appropriate on two levels: *santral* in Turkish means both "control center or headquarters" and "power plant", and Santralistanbul wants to be both of these – the center of Turkey's burgeoning art scene as well as a powerful source of inspiration.

View from the Galata Bridge of the New Town sprawling to the north of the Bosphorus. The Galata Tower, a welcoming relic of days long gone, dominates the many new boutiques, clubs, restaurants and galleries.

BEYOND THE GOLDEN HORN: THE NEW TOWN AND THE EUROPEAN SIDE OF THE BOSPHORUS

The strategically important district north of the capital's Golden Horn was annexed during the reign of East Roman Emperor Theodosius II (401–450). Genoese merchants settled here later on, and the Beyoğlu district – itself divided into smaller *machallas* or "neighborhoods", such as Karaköy (Galata), Tophane and Taksim – is today the modern heart of the city, beating loud and fast. Financial districts soar up in the adjacent northeastern districts of Şişli and Beşiktas demonstrating a city in the midst of change. Those who like things a bit quieter should follow the Bosphorus further up to Sarıyer.

BEYOND THE GOLDEN HORN: THE NEW TOWN AND THE EUROPEAN SIDE OF THE BOSPHORUS

The port district between the Golden Horn and Galata Tower is today known as Karaköy or "black village" – after the house façades which were blackened by the smoke of old steam ferries. The similarly common name of Galata refers to an early Celtic (Gallic) settlement. The area around the Galata Bridge on the northern banks of the Golden Horn is a particular hive of activity, with metro, tram and bus lines all converging not far from the ferry terminal. To the west of the bridge, an early-morning fish market is held on the crowded square between the dock, workshops and ware-

Somewhat neglected in recent decades, the Tophane district is becoming increasingly popular, especially among Istanbul's younger citizens. This is particularly due to the booming art scene and the many galleries established here, as well as the numerous cafés and restaurants with outdoor seating where one can relax and smoke a shisha (right and top). Things are more hectic at the fish market in Karaköy (above).

houses, while to the east lies the cruise ship terminal, from which boats head off along the Bosphorus and out to sea. Continuing onto the north-east is the Tophane district, named after a former cannon foundry (Turkish: *tophane*) and which has been experiencing a revival of sorts in recent years.

"Here, anyone can live peacefully beneath their fig tree and vines", wrote the rabbi Isaac Zarfati during the days of the Ottoman Empire to the Jewish communities of Central Europe in 1470. Although the history of Judaism in Turkey dates back as far as the third century BC, most Jews living in the country today are Sephardic Jews who ultimately followed Zarfati's beckoning call – they are descendents of the Jews banished from the Iberian Peninsula as a result of the Reconquista in the 15th century. According to the information from the Jewish community, some 26,000 Jews today live in Turkey – more than in any other Muslim country. Most of them, around 20,000, reside in Istanbul, whose Jewish community was once among the largest in the world. However, it is barely visible in everyday Turkish life; very rarely does one hear old Ladino – the traditional Romance language of

JEWISH LIFE UNDER
THE CRESCENT MOON

the Sephardic Jews, which is related to Spanish like Yiddish is related to German. The history of of the Jewish odyssey from Spain to Turkey and of their subsequent lives in Turkey is documented in Turkey's first Jewish Museum, which was opened in a former synagogue in Karaköy in 2001.

The city has nineteen synagogues (left: the Italian synagogue in Galata; top: the Maallem synagogue in Hasköy), three of which are only open in summer. Above: Chief Rabbi Ishak Haleva speaks in the Neve Shalom synagogue, situated just a few minutes' walk north-west of the Galata Tower, and one of the largest Jewish places of worship in Turkey – it has been the target of three terrorist attacks, in 1986, 1992 and 2003.

BEYOND THE GOLDEN HORN: THE NEW TOWN AND THE EUROPEAN SIDE OF THE BOSPHORUS

Istanbul's art scene is booming. Those wanting to get a good overview of the latest developments should head to the former 19th-century warehouse located right by the Bosphorus, not far from where the large cruise ships moor in the port of Karaköy. In December 2004, the Istanbul Modern Museum opened here as the first Turkish museum of contemporary art. The exhibitions are spread over an area of 8,000 sq m (86,080 sq ft) and specialize in modern Turkish painting and sculpture. The permanent exhibition on the upper floor (laid out by theme, not chronologically) is reserved

for these. The ground floor houses temporary exhibitions by artists from Turkey's regions and from other countries, as well as photography and new media (video, digital). All the works are shown in their social, cultural, economic, and political context. The museum also has a cinema.

The museum was primarily made possible by the private initiative of the Eczacıbaşı family, who owns Turkey's largest pharmaceutical company. Their private collection forms the basis of the permanent exhibit, which displays works by all major Turkish artists of the last 150 years. Left: Ekrem Yalcindag, who was born in the Turkish town of Gölbaşi and now resides in Germany, named his painting (oil on canvas) *374 Farben* ("374 colors").

In December 2010, a newspaper reported that biennials would rain over the planet "like shooting stars". They stated that there were already more than 200 worldwide, and that the biggest problem with "the popular surprise packages" is that "they shine so brightly but, alas, are extinguished so quickly". The "Remembering Istanbul" conference provided a good opportunity for reflection to kick off the 12th Biennial in 2011: it has now been around 25 years since the first Istanbul Biennial was held in 1987. "Contemporary Art in Traditional Spaces" was the motto at the time, and the same motto could, essentially, still apply to the present-day international art show, held regularly every two years. The way in which it explores the (varying) "rooms", ranging from the old bonded warehouse, to the cistern, to the Hagia Sophia itself, and the way in which it deals with the

"What keeps mankind alive?" was the question, from Brecht's *Threepenny Opera*, at the 11th Istanbul Biennial in 2009 (all pictures). The question as to what keeps art alive was answered by the list of sponsors in the exhibition catalogue. Critics complained about the "exclusive" nature of the political art at the Biennial, which is organized by a private foundation but co-financed by the Turkish government – the gilded cage of the exhibition hall.

SHOOTING STARS ABOVE THE GILDED CAGE OF ART: ISTANBUL BIENNIAL

global (and globalized) world of art, demonstrate how much Istanbul continues to be shaped by cultural, religious, ethnic and social extremes. But it also demonstrates that people are more than willing to face these polar opposites – even if as a showcase of bright shooting stars held every two years.

BEYOND THE GOLDEN HORN: THE NEW TOWN AND THE EUROPEAN SIDE OF THE BOSPHORUS

Two fine mosques are located near the cruise ship terminal in the port of Karaköy at the start of the Bosphorus: the mosque founded by Grand Admiral Kılıç Ali Paşa (1519–1587) in 1580 is one of the most interesting latter works by master builder Sinan, who, based on the same floor plan and vault structure, once again used the Hagia Sophia as his model. The rather cheerless interior is however decorated with beautiful Iznik faïence ceramics.

Looming up just a few hundred yards farther north-east are the two elegant minarets of the Nusretiye Mosque. It was built between 1823 and 1826

by Armenian architect Krikor Amira Balyan (1764–1831) on behalf of Sultan Mahmut II (1785–1839), as part of a larger project to rebuild the Tophane artillery barracks and a permanent memento of his victory over the Janissaries – which also explains the building's name ("Victory Mosque").

When Kılıç Ali Paşa ordered the construction of the mosque that was to bear his name (top), it stood right by the waters of the Bosphorus. It is no coincidence that the Nusretiye Mosque (above and left) overlooks the Selimiye Mosque on the opposite shores of the Bosphorus: it is there that the reformist sultan stationed his troops, which replaced the old Janissary corps and whose organization was based on the European model.

BEYOND THE GOLDEN HORN: THE NEW TOWN AND THE EUROPEAN SIDE OF THE BOSPHORUS

Where the striking Galata Tower stands today a predecessor building dating from the fifth and sixth centuries is said to have stood. The present-day tower, a solid circular structure with a conical tin roof, has soared above the rooftops of the New Town since 1348, acting as the district's main land-mark. At that time, it marked the highest point of the defense wall which the Genoese had built around their commercial settlement of Galata. Originally erected as a watch-tower, the building, which had been damaged several times over the centuries by fires, storms and earthquakes, but

The Galata Tower, once also known as the "Tower of Christ", is the only one to remain of the twenty-four watchtowers erected by the Genoese to protect their commercial settlement on the Golden Horn. The well-fortified structure also withstood the destruction of the remaining Genoese fortress walls during the mid-19th century. The square around the tower, with its many eateries, is popular with tourists and locals alike.

had always been restored, also served as a Janissary post, prison, observatory and – until well into the 1960s – as a fire station. Today, the two top floors house restaurants. The wrap-around balcony provides fine panoramic views over the Beyoğlu district, the Bosphorus and the Golden Horn.

Just like New York, Istanbul too is a city which never sleeps; at least not in its trendiest and most modern part. Also known as "Downtown Istanbul", this is where every A-lister likes to see and be seen: in Beyoğlu. There is a wide selection of bars, discos and nightclubs in the small alleyways around the Istiklal Caddesi shopping street and also around Taksim Square. This is where Istanbul – and indeed Turkey – displays its more Western, open-minded side. And those who can't afford the clubs can also drink raki, dance and entertain themselves in a less expensive pub or simple music bar. The "Babylon" (at Sehbender Sokak 3) is a well-known institution for live performances: whether it be hip hop, (Turkish) pop or (American) jazz, there is something here to suit every taste (as well as free-flowing beer from the bottle). The nights are similarly long and lively at the Roxy dance and performance club

In the heart of Istanbul's nightlife: Beyoğlu is the perfect place for men, women, straight and gay people to enjoy themselves – even if this is just at one of the many street cafés. Fatih Akin's documentary, *Crossing the Bridge*, provides an insight into the music metropolis on the Bosphorus, while the best place for clubbers and scensters to find out the latest information once in the city is, *Time Out Istanbul*, an English-language guide.

YOUNG AND EASY-GOING: NIGHTLIFE IN ISTANBUL

(at Aslan Yatağı Sokak 5; anyone who dines in the YAN Gastrobar beforehand may access the club for free without any bouncers via a side entrance). Those who prefer movies (usually in Turkish with subtitles) will also find beautiful old cinema complexes, such as the Atlas, on the Istiklal Caddesi.

For Islamic Studies specialist Annemarie Schimmel, it was mysticism which particularly characterized Islam – whose inner, spiritual life was at risk of drowning in the "fine network of dogmatic distinctions … in the increasingly extrinsic legal regulations". Sufism is an expression of mystical yearning, whose early followers, similar to the Christian ascetics in the Middle East, wore dark hair shirts made from wool (Arabic: *suf*). The first Dervish orders (Persian: *darwiš*, meaning "beggar") were already emerging in the 12th century, as religious brotherhoods who dedicated their lives to Sufism.

The Galata Mevlevihanesi Museum, the Whirling Dervish Hall and officially the Museum of Divan Literature pays tribute to Jalal ad-Din Rumi (1207–1273), the most famous poet in Islamic mysticism and founder of the Mevlevi Dervish Order, who spent almost half a century teaching in the town of Konya.

The museum is housed in a building situated near the Tünel mountain station, where Istanbul's first Dervish monastery was founded in 1492. It was reconstructed after burning down in the second half of the 18th century. The Sufis, who refer to the founder of their Order as Mevlevi (or Mevlana, meaning "Sir", "Lord"), perform their ceremonial twirling dance (Turkish: *sema*) in the octagonal Whirling Dervish Hall.

BEYOND THE GOLDEN HORN: THE NEW TOWN AND THE EUROPEAN SIDE OF THE BOSPHORUS

The train operating from the valley station in Karaköy on the banks of the Golden Horn, through a tunnel and up to the Tünel station on Galata Hill is only a subway insofar as it runs underground. It is actually a funicular railway built by French engineer Henri Gavant between 1871 and 1874, which performed its maiden trip on 17 January 1875. It was converted to running with an electric engine in the mid-20th century, and today transports an average of 5.4 million passengers a year.

Istiklal Caddesi ("Independence Avenue") is one of the best-known shopping streets in the

Beyoğlu district, visited by around 3 million people a day at weekends. It starts at the Tünel mountain station, and the farther one ambles down the street, the closer one gets to the main center of nightlife, with bars, clubs and restaurants. There is no lock-out here – night simply becomes day.

A nostalgic tram jingles its way down the Istiklal Caddesi (left), which is otherwise a pedestrian zone with many different food stalls (above) and cafés. A ride on the Tünel railway, whose carriages were redesigned in 2007 (top), lasts exactly one minute and twenty seconds. The train is named after the "micro district" of Tünel in Beyoğlu, made up of a few tiny alleyways.

It was two merchants, Hakim from Aleppo and Schems from Damascus, who opened the city's first coffeehouse in 1554 – with a fountain at the center and sofas placed along the walls. This was where the men came to play backgammon, chat or listen to the *meddah* or storyteller. These sorts of coffeehouses soon also became popular meeting places for artists and intellectuals in the mid-19th century, and coffeehouses as well as the fashion for drinking coffee quickly spread all around Europe.

Traditional Turkish coffee is prepared by boiling finely ground coffee powder with a little *(az sekerli)* or much more *(sekerli)* sugar in a long-handled, slightly conical copper pot. It is then served unfiltered in small cups for which no spoon is required, as the coffee grounds should remain on the bottom of the cup. Perhaps surprisingly, Turkey's actual national drink, however, is not coffee, but tea.

STRONG AND DARK: TURKISH COFFEE AND TEA

The traditional preparation method follows the Russian samovar principle of heating in two pots, known as *semaver* in Turkish, which fit on top of one another. The attractive tulip-shaped glasses in which the tea is ultimately served keep the delicious, amber beverage hot for a long time.

Turkish coffee (above) should traditionally be as black as hell and as sweet as love, and its grounds can be used to tell the future. To do this, the saucer is placed on the cup, which is turned upside down and then tipped back to its original position – after which all you need is a little imagination. But whether it be coffee or tea (left), make sure you have enough time to enjoy it properly – and maybe even try a shisha (top).

BEYOND THE GOLDEN HORN: THE NEW TOWN AND THE EUROPEAN SIDE OF THE BOSPHORUS

Opinions are divided on the Nevizade Sokak, an entertainment strip running parallel to the Istiklal Caddesi: those who like it loud and lively will love the hustle and bustle around the closely packed tables and the throng of traveling artists, hawkers and street musicians. Others avoid the area, deeming it to an overpriced tourist trap. The goings on in Çiçek Passage are similarly hectic: large hanging baskets filled with vivid geraniums, trailing petunias and ivy dangle from pretty glass roofs, epitomizing the name (Çiçek Pasajı = "flower passage"), although the pubs and restaurants make it hard to

imagine the times when this was one of the most distinguished addresses in imperial Istanbul. It is perhaps more interesting to visit the nearby Balık Pazarı, a vibrant fish and vegetable market. Most restaurants buy their octopus, calamari, shrimp, grouper and other "fruits of the sea" here.

"They ensconce themselves in the wine houses and beer halls or in the worst kind of pubs, where the atmosphere is very cheerful but also very raucous", wrote French author Pierre Loti, whose first novel *Aziyadé* (1876) was set in Istanbul. He summed things up thus, "everywhere you look, people are drinking, singing, playing and dancing", which is still very much in evidence even today (left and above: Nevizade Sokak, top: Çiçek Passage).

When the Pera Palace was opened in 1892, it was considered the finest property in the city – appointed with every imaginable comfort and finery. It was the first building in Istanbul to have electric lighting, running hot water and a guest elevator. The palace boasted marble from Carrara, hand-knotted carpets and silk drapes, and was owned by the operators of the Orient Express, who transported their illustrious, wealthy guests in ritzy first-class sleeper carriages from Paris to Istanbul, where there had previously never been such a luxurious place to stay. It was also these illustrious guests who gave the hotel its legendary status: residents have included Josephine Baker, Sarah Bernhardt, Marlene Dietrich and Mata Hari, Alfred Hitchcock, Jacqueline Kennedy and Queen Elizabeth II, to name but a few. And there was also Greta Garbo, who spent twenty-one days in the

A HOTEL LEGEND CUM "MUSEUM HOTEL": PERA PALACE

hotel in 1924 – the exact room is unknown, which is why, to make things easier, every room in the north-eastern corner is named after her. Agatha Christie is said to have written parts of her legendary novel, *Murder on the Orient Express*, in Room 411 – in stately surroundings, of course.

The present-day Beyoğlu district was still called "Pera" (Greek, meaning "opposite") until well into the 20th century because it lies on the opposite side of the Golden Horn as seen from Istanbul's Old Town. The Pera Palace had long rested too much on its laurels – until it was closed for extensive renovations in 2008 and reopened in September 2010. Its new (luxury) category it is now a "museum hotel".

Not every hotel has been able to boost its legendary prestige like the Pera Palace (which is not to be confused with the Pera Museum). Some simply disappear, for example the Bristol Hotel, built on Meşrutiyet Caddesi (running parallel to the Istiklal Caddesi shopping street on the western side) in 1893 and based on the plans of Greek architect Achille Manoussos. It was purchased by members of the Koçes family of Turkish industrialists, through the Suna & Inan Kıraç Foundation in 2002, and restored to such an extent over the next three years that, in June 2005, a new museum, rather than

the refurbished old hotel, was opened there instead. The collection, largely compiled by Suna and Inan Kiraç, is now centered around more than 300 paintings by Turkish and European painters, including Osman Hamdi Bey's *Tortoise Trainer*, which was valued at 3.5 million U.S. dollars.

The (art) world is Istanbul's guest: while the lower floors of the museum (above: the entrance) display a painting collection on everyday life in the Ottoman Empire (the painting on the left was created by an unknown artist in the 18th century) and a cultural history exhibition, the upper levels are reserved for temporary exhibits (top: Colombian Fernando Botero in front of his paintings).

In Istanbul, those with a sweet tooth don't have to wait for their desserts – they'll find the sweetest of tempting treats all over the city. *Baklava*, a pastry soaked in syrup and filled with chopped walnuts, almonds or pistachios, is the first that comes to mind. Add to this a cup of very strong mocha and you'll have more than enough to keep you going for a while. *Helva*, a weightwatcher's nightmare made from wheat flour, sesame oil, honey and sugar, is just as sticky and sweet. And there is good reason why *lokum*, a syrup made from jellied starch and sugar with pistachios or almonds, is known to English speakers as Turkish Delight – nowhere else are these sweet "bites" (*lokma* in Turkish) as delicious as they are there. Or how about *tavuk gögsü kazandibi*, a milk pudding made with chopped chicken breast and rice flour? Marzipan in all its forms is another popular Turkish confec-

tion. And we certainly mustn't forget another sweet made from dried fruit, rose water, cinnamon and beans, which Noah himself is said to have invented using what was left of his supplies once he had finally withstood the Deluge: *aşure* – possibly the sweetest reason for living in the here and now.

La Dolce Vita in Istanbul: the range of sweet dishes is as tempting as the goods displayed in the respective stores (top: a honey shop on Istiklal Caddesi). The wealth of new creations is endless, including for example a string of chopped almonds or pistachios dunked several times in concentrated, hot grape juice to make the "sweet sausage". Anyone who worries about the calories only has themselves to blame …

The square was named after a historic water distribution system (Turkish: *taksim*), which was the first building to emerge here in 1732. The water was sourced from the dams in the Belgrade Forest (in the Sarıyer district in the north of Istanbul) via a long-distance water pipe. It was collected there until the second half of the 19th century and distributed to the public wells of the lower-lying districts. Some of the surrounding palaces, such as the Yildiz Palace, also had a direct supply. Today, the small, octagonal building of the water distribution system marks the northern end of Istiklal

The square's most eye-catching feature is the "Monument of the Republic", created by Italian artist Pietro Canonica and unveiled on 8 August 1928. It portrays the country's founder, Mustafa Kemal Atatürk, in civilian clothing on the south-facing side (right) and in military uniform on the north-facing side. The square is lined by buildings such as the Atatürk Cultural Center and the 96-m (315-ft) Marmara Hotel (top).

Caddesi and the terminus of the tram running along this busy shopping street. The square itself, a highly frequented traffic hub where the city's main arteries converge, symbolizes the urban heart of modern Istanbul. Metros, bus lines and an underground funicular railway all stop here.

Unlike the exact date of Atatürk's birth, his death date is recorded down to the last minute: every 10 November at precisely 9.05 a.m., the traffic comes to a total standstill right around the country, and people get out of their cars to pay tribute to someone who has been described as a great strategist as a soldier and as a visionary as the founder of a nation. His reforms – the abolition of the caliphate, the banishment of religion from the public domain and equal rights for women, as well as the introduction of the Roman alphabet and the Gregorian calendar – constituted a radical break with the past. The man who was instrumental in founding the Republic of Turkey in 1923 was born in early 1881 in the Ottoman town of Saloniki (today the northern Greek city of Thessaloniki) as the son of customs officer Ali Rıza and his wife Zübeyde, a farmer's daughter. The couple named their child Mustafa – family names

The image of Mustafa Kemal Atatürk (1881–1938; above: with the traditional lambskin hat, right: with the modern hat he later ordered every man to wear) is omnipresent; his political legacy has shaped the country, and his success as general of the Turkish army made him a national hero, who actually ended up as a sole ruler. Top right: The museum room dedicated to Atatürk in the Pera Palace Hotel.

were not common at the time. A teacher pleased with his academic results later gave him the additional name of Kemal (the Arabic word for "completion"). The Republic of Turkey was proclaimed on 29 October 1923, Kemal named himself Atatürk ("the father of Turkey") from 1934 to his death in 1938.

The Dolmabahçe Palace was to be for the New Town what the Topkapı Palace was for the Old Town: an excessive architectural allegory for the power and glory of the increasingly westernized Ottoman Empire, whose star was nevertheless waning in the 19th century. The country, which had been weak- ened economically by uprisings in the European territories, was ridiculed as the "Sick Man on the Bosphorus" and was at risk of becoming a pawn of foreign powers. But that did not stop Sultan Abdülmecit I (1823– 1861) from commissioning the construction of a monumental palace in 1843. The location

chosen was the raised garden (Turkish: *dolma bahçe*) created by his predecessors, Sultans Ahmet I and Osman II – a silted-up bay on the shores of the Bosphorus, where a summer residence had been erected as in the 1600s (burned down in 1840). Today it is one of the most visited sites in the city.

The approximately 45,000-sq-m (484,200-sq-ft) L-shaped palace complex was built over thirteen years and sprawls for more than 600 m (1,968 ft) along the banks of the Bosphorus (top; left: the staircase; above: the ceremonial hall with the 4.5-tonne/4.95-ton chandelier). The Ottoman sultans resided here until proclamation of the Turkish Republic in 1923; Kemal Atatürk also resided in the palace from time to time, and died there in 1938.

"We Turks love living close to the edge", said Fatih Terim, after the Turkish national team he had coached for a record period since the summer of 2005 was eliminated from the qualification tournament for the 2010 World Cup in South Africa with a 0:2 loss against Belgium on 10 October 2009.

Terim scored 129 goals during his playing career as a defender for Galatasaray Istanbul (1974 to 1985), and was then given the presumably flattering nickname of *imparator* ("emperor") after gaining experience as a coach in Florence and Milan. Just one year prior, Terim had been named "coach of the tournament" when the Turkish team lost a close game against Germany during the 2008 European championships in Austria and Switzerland. But he was now resigning and ending his glorious career, and his description of the "edge" proves the height from which not only coaches and players

of the Turkish national team have to fall, but also those of the new Turkish premier league – the "Süper Lig", sponsored by the Turkish sports betting agency Spor Toto since August 2010. Eighteen teams compete in this annually for the championship, and for a (usually well-paid) life on the edge …

Ever since the "Süper Lig" was founded by the Turkish football association in 1959, the "big three" – the Bosphorus-based top teams Galatasaray Istanbul, Fenerbahçe Istanbul and Beşiktaş Istanbul – have more or less shared the spoils among themselves. Today, the city has five premier league teams – with Istanbul Büyükşehir Belediyespor and Kasımpaşaspor in addition to the three named above.

BEYOND THE GOLDEN HORN: THE NEW TOWN AND THE EUROPEAN SIDE OF THE BOSPHORUS

The "Star Palace" (Yıldız Sarayı) completed at the start of the 20th century and comprising a main palace, as well as several pavilions and villas scattered over vast parklands, was used by Sultan Abdülhamit II (1842–1918) as a luxurious refuge after he no longer felt safe in the Dolmabahçe Palace. As the sultan lived in constant fear of being attacked, he had a high wall built around the palace, and a few thousand soldiers barracked on the vast grounds to protect his life.

At the Çırağan Palace, meanwhile, which has been converted from the immense sultan's residence to a ritzy hotel, it is the

Despite the lengths to which Sultan Abdülhamit II (top right: Yildiz Palace) went to cocoon himself, he barely survived an attack in 1905, and was eventually overthrown by the "Young Turks", a national Turkish reformist party formed in 1876 and oriented around Western ideology, in 1909. Above and right: Looming up to the east of the Dolmabahçe Palace is the Çırağan Palace, restored as a luxury hotel in the early 1990s.

guest who is always the king today. The complex, built by Nikoğos Balyan on the orders of Sultan Abdülaziz (1830–1876) is now the Çiragan Palace Kempinski, a five-star hotel and spa, and anyone who has ever wanted to be a sultan can live out their dream of luxury and opulence here.

Orhan Pamuk, born in Istanbul on 7 June 1952, was awarded the Nobel Prize for Literature in 2006, the first Turkish citizen to have received this accolade. In his acceptance speech he recounted how he decided to drop everything and become a writer at the age of twenty-two. In this same speech, he also revealed his "secret of writing": tenacity and patience. The fact that he referred back to an old Turkish saying – "to dig a well with a needle" – is probably just as indicative of the author's character as it is of the modesty with which he describes his art as a craft. He himself originally wanted to become a painter, and this is evident in his book *Istanbul: Memories and the City*, which combines his own life story with a touching declaration of love for his home town, and in his detective story *My Name is Red*. His acceptance speech continued: "When I ... told of old Persian miniature painters

ORHAN PAMUK: "TO DIG A WELL WITH A NEEDLE"

who, over years of passionate work, constantly drew the same horse until they could picture it with their eyes closed, I realized that I was actually talking about the career of a writer, and about my life." In 2010, he got the Norman Mailer Lifetime Achievement Award in the United States.

Orhan Pamuk (top: at the Nobel Prize-giving ceremony in Stockholm in 2006; above: in his Istanbul study, left: after a reading) studied architecture and journalism before starting his career as a writer. His work, published in over 100 countries, earned him many literary awards, as well as the Peace Prize of the German Book Trade in 2005 and an honorary doctorate from Yale in 2010.

BEYOND THE GOLDEN HORN: THE NEW TOWN AND THE EUROPEAN SIDE OF THE BOSPHORUS

Two bridges span the Bosphorus, whose name is derived from the Turkish word *boğaziçi*, meaning "throat, gullet or strait". Sprawling in the shadow of the older, 1,510-m-long (4,954-ft) "First Bosphorus Bridge", built between 1970 and 1973, is Ortaköy, a once quiet fishing village which, in recent decades, has developed into a not-so-quiet district of Istanbul boasting beautiful gardens and great nightlife. The weekends are a particularly popular time for the city slickers to flock here to visit the many art galleries, cafés, pubs and nightclubs around the docks, which are also frequented

With its colorful houses in narrow alleyways, and numerous bars and cafés, Ortaköy has an almost Mediterranean feel. Although the alleyways around the mosque really come to life on Sundays with a vibrant flea and farmer's market ideal for ambling, browsing and buying, the place is also worth a visit any other day of the week, when you can relax and soak up the atmosphere while glancing out to the Bosphorus.

by many students. The lively center of all this activity is Iskele Square by the pier, where fishermen previously used to unload their daily catch. On Sundays, you can also visit a market here offering a regional culinary specialty, *kumpir* – baked potatoes filled with curd cheese, mince or vegetables.

BEYOND THE GOLDEN HORN: THE NEW TOWN AND THE EUROPEAN SIDE OF THE BOSPHORUS

Ortaköy is symbolized by the Büyük Mecidiye Mosque, better known as the Ortaköy Mosque, which sits idyllically atop a rocky outcrop. Its construction began in 1854, to the designs of architect Nikoğos Balyan, who, together with his father Karabet, is also responsible for the Dolmabahçe Palace complex. The domed central structure, held in the Ottoman baroque style, is flanked by four corner turrets with neo-baroque roofs; two slender, elegant minarets rise up from the adjoining two-floor building. The mosque was commissioned by Sultan Abdülmecid I (1823–1861),

who had succeeded his father on 1 July 1839. Inside the mosque you can admire some superb Arabic calligraphy created by Sultan Abdülmecid (1839–1861) himself. Just next to the mosque is a lovely tea garden, ideal for relaxing, perhaps smoking a shisha, and letting your mind wander.

The light-filled interior (above) of the mosque, with its marble-lined prayer room, large windows and low-hanging crystal chandelier, is reminiscent of a small baroque palace. The view of the building (left), which crouches in the shadow of the First Bosphorus Bridge, is a "classic", which every traveler cruising northward on the Bosphorus from Karaköy toward the Black Sea can enjoy.

The Bosphorus is an "expression of what we have in Istanbul", said football sage Christoph Daum in an interview for German-French television broadcaster ARTE, "something which connects and divides". And he knew exactly what he was talking about: As a coach of the Fenerbahçe Istanbul club, based on the Asian side, he won the Turkish championship in 2004 and 2005 – a feat he had also been able to achieve as early as 1995 while working with Beşiktaş Istanbul on the European side. Yet when he narrowly missed out on the championship while back under contract at Fenerbahçe Istanbul in 2010, he needed the police to escort him from the stadium. On the one hand, this demonstrates the fanaticism – not entirely foreign to other nations either – of some football supporters, who would do well to remember the quote by another knowledgeable football great

The 31-km-long (19-mile), 660 to 3,000-m-wide (2,165 to 9,843-ft) and 30 to 120-m-deep (98 to 394-ft) strait between Europe and Asia, which connects the Black Sea with the Sea of Marmara, is named after Zeus, the father of the gods, who transformed his lover, Io, into a white cow to trick his wife. Suspicious, the wife sent a horsefly to chase the cow through the strait, which has been known as the Bosphorus ("Cow's passage") ever since.

innocuously born in Italy: "Football is ding, dang and dong. It's not just ding" (Giovanni Trapattoni). And on the other, it does nothing to change the fact that Daum is totally right about the Bosphorus: it has both a connecting and a dividing character. Sometimes more so, sometimes less so.

BEYOND THE GOLDEN HORN: THE NEW TOWN AND THE EUROPEAN SIDE OF THE BOSPHORUS

Barge rides to the "pleasure resorts" on the Bosphorus – as Turkish poet Mehmet Tevfik (1843–1893) called them – were once only reserved for the wealthy. It was not until the 19th century that paddle steamers built in England began to cruise along the strait, and even then this was initially only permitted for men. As there were no suitable piers, the passengers had to switch to rowboats, which people (men) feared would compromise the ladies' grace and femininity! Today, these sorts of problems are thankfully a thing of the past. Every day, cruise ships travel up and

North of Arnavutköy (right), the journey continues on to Bebek (top), where cafés and restaurants by the pier invite visitors to stop by, relax and enjoy the most delicious fish dishes and the sweetest of desserts. Intellectual food for thought, on the other hand, is served up by the English-language Boğaziçi University, whose building sprawls in front of the Second Bosphorus Bridge, also known as the Fatih Sultan Mehmet Bridge.

down the Bosphorus, past magnificent summer palaces, wealthy Ottoman mansions, lush parklands and idyllic historic Bosphorus villages, such as Arnavutköy and Bebek, whose picturesque yacht marinas and beautifully painted wooden houses exude an almost Mediterranean feel.

"Hills with wooded valleys rise up on both sides of the Bosphorus. Vineyards, tropical fruit trees, flowers and herbs all co-exist in glorious harmony. And running down these hills on both sides are around thirty crystal-clear streams. This and the many bays forming the Bosphorus are what make the surrounding region not simply one of the most homely, but also one of the most beautiful". These were the gushing words written by the French humanist and Istanbul resident Pierre Gilles between 1544 and 1550 to describe the strait dividing Europe and Asia. He made sure to add that even the Greek mythological hero, Jason (of the Argonauts), "declared these shores an abode of the gods". It could also be mentioned that these gods were followed by the Ottomans – or in any case their high-ranking dignitaries and other distinguished people. The legacy they left behind on the shores

One of the best preserved wooden villas on the European side of the upper Bosphorus is the Sait Halim Paşa Yalısı (right): Today appointed with all the amenities of a modern luxury hotel, guests can now choose between "normal" luxury rooms and, in keeping with the atmosphere, a "king's suite". Top: The Serişer Yalısı, situated farther north on the European side oft he straits, in Sarıyer, is open to the public as a museum.

"YALIS": TRADITIONAL WOODEN VILLAS ON THE BOSPHORUS

of the Bosphorus can be witnessed in the truest sense of the word even today. A *yalı* is the name given to their beautiful summer residences, found on both the European and Asian sides of the strait: grand wooden villas with overhanging roofs, built right on the water's edge, each with its own pier.

BEYOND THE GOLDEN HORN: THE NEW TOWN AND THE EUROPEAN SIDE OF THE BOSPHORUS

A mighty fortress, Rumeli Hisarı, dominates the view just beyond Bebek's riverside promenade, situated farther north up the Bosphorus toward the next promontory on the European side. It was built in 1452, some nine months before the conquest of Constantinople, on the orders of Sultan Mehmet II (Fatih). And as history has shown, the conqueror's plans bore fruit: to control the Bosphorus together with the Anadolu Hisarı fortress built by Sultan Bayezit I on the opposite, Asian side in 1395, and to thus cut off supplies to the Byzantines. After the Fall of Constantinople, the

fortress had fulfilled its purpose and was then used as a state prison. It was partly destroyed by an earthquake and later a fire. Today, it houses a museum, and is also known as a particularly atmospheric backdrop and open-air theater for concerts and the festival held here every summer.

The Conqueror resorted to a ruse to ensure the Rumeli Hisarı building of the fortress was completed as quickly as possible: he entrusted a section each to three of his commanders, which prompted fierce competition and meant that the entire building, with its three large round towers and thirteen smaller towers, and which sprawls up a wooded slope on the European side of the Bosphorus, was completed in just four months.

BEYOND THE GOLDEN HORN: THE NEW TOWN AND THE EUROPEAN SIDE OF THE BOSPHORUS

Just like the First Bosphorus Bridge, opened fifteen years earlier some 5 km (3 miles) farther south, so the Second Bosphorus Bridge, officially approved for traffic on 3 July 1988, and which bears the name of Sultan Mehmet II (Fatih), is also a suspension bridge. It was built at the point along the Bosphorus which happens to be its narrowest, at some 660 m (2,165 ft) wide and where, in 512 BC, Persian King Darius I destroyed a "floating bridge" (pontoon bridge) over the water during his legendary crusade against the Scythians. Its much more modern variant, measuring

With its clearance height (the distance between the bottom edge of the roadway support and the sea level) of 64 m (210 ft), the bridge is also tall enough for oil tankers, aircraft carriers and cruise ships to pass beneath it. To reduce the traffic volume in future, the "Marmaray Project" is currently in progress – an earthquake-proof tunnel under the Bosphorus to take the traffic from West to East at a depth of 56 m (184 ft) below sea level.

FATIH SULTAN MEHMET BRIDGE (SECOND BOSPHORUS BRIDGE) 54

1,510 m (4,954 ft) in length (main span width between the pylons: 1,090 m/3,576 ft), has a 39.4-m-wide (129-ft) roadway with eight lanes and two emergency lanes. Like its southern counterpart, it is also a toll road, and is barely able to cope with the volume of daily traffic between West and East.

Istanbul is booming: as the 2010 European Capital of Culture and also as an extremely vibrant trading and financial center straddling two continents. One in five Turks today lives in the metropolis on the Bosphorus – so it is no wonder that ever more state-of-the-art skyscrapers soar up in many parts of the incessant sprawl that is an Istanbul bursting at the seams. These give the place the look and feel of a megacity, whose heavenward-bound skyline should be as far removed from the old, predominantly ancient and Ottoman townscape around the Topkapı as it actually is in years. Apart from the architectural challenge of being located on a faultline and thus in an area at high risk of earthquakes due to tectonic activity in the Sea of Marmara, traffic planning in particular requires a lot of skill and effort: it is hoped that the threat of gridlock will be erased with the "Marmaray Rail Tube Tunnel

and Commuter Rail Mass Transit System" – currently one of the largest-ever traffic-related projects in the world. Apart from building the spectacular tunnel structure under the Bosphorus, it also involves expanding and upgrading the rail network as part of the "Railway vision" initiative.

When it comes to building increasingly taller skyscrapers, the financial district of Maslak (left and above) in the Şişli area of modern Istanbul leads the way. This is where, among other structures, the "Diamond of Istanbul" stands, Turkey's highest skyscraper at 270 m tall (886 ft), soaring toward the heavens. The skyline of Levent (top), another finance district also in the Şişli area, adjacent to Maslak, has similarly spellbinding towers.

BEYOND THE GOLDEN HORN: THE NEW TOWN AND THE EUROPEAN SIDE OF THE BOSPHORUS

Back on the Bosphorus, far away from the soaring new buildings of the Şişli district, quieter areas like Sarıyer make one feel as if one has been transported back to the olden days. Listening to the waves which lap incessantly at the shore, and which seem to almost symbolize the way things go in general, one may be forgiven for having too idyllic an impression of these times. They were once probably not quite so idyllic, especially when one thinks of the old practice of "district raids" *(mahalle baskını)*, which Klaus Kreiser describes in his historic Istanbul city guide. In those days it was

Every day, fishermen set off from Sarıyer and head up the Bosphorus, not far from the Black Sea, flinging their nets into the water and reeling in their catches, some of which end up at the seafood restaurants at the port. Sarıyer, incidentally is not only the name of the fishing village, a small town in its own right, but also that of one of Istanbul's thirty-nine city district – twenty-five on the European side and fourteen on the Asian side.

quite possible for a man to be approached by a veiled woman on the Galata Bridge and, hoping for an amorous adventure, being lured to a house in the Sarıyer district. There, however, he would not be robbed of his senses or money – but was instead told off by disgusted guardians of public morals.

A fish market in Üsküdar: around one-third of Istanbul's population – a total of 14 to 16 million according to estimates by Istanbul's traffic experts – live on the Asian side of the city, and two-thirds on the European side.

THE OTHER SIDE OF THE BOSPHORUS: THE ASIAN PART OF THE CITY

From Europe to Asia in less than half an hour? That's not a problem in Istanbul: it only takes about twenty minutes to cross the Bosphorus by ferry, moving from one continent to the other – and there are ferry terminals at Eminönü and Karaköy on the European side and Kadıköy and Üsküdar on the Asian side. It is certainly worth visiting these two Asian districts if, as a tourist, you fancy going beyond the attractions on the European side alone. Both were once cities in their own right and now form the heart of the Asian side. True explorers, however, also indulge in a daytrip to the Princes' Islands in the Sea of Marmara.

THE OTHER SIDE OF THE BOSPHORUS: THE ASIAN PART OF THE CITY

Those wanting not just to cross from West to East, but to also enjoy the entire length of the Bosphorus (going back and forth between the continents) should take a ride on one of the passenger ships mooring in Eminönü; the entire journey lasts around six hours. Their last port of call on the Asian side is Anadolu Kavağı on the upper Bosphorus, not far from its mouth onto the Black Sea, where travelers generally stop for one to three hours before returning to Eminönü. Originally a fishing village and still known for its fine seafood restaurants even today, it is worth taking a half-hour walk to the ruins of

Traditional life on the Bosphorus: fishing boats calmly bob up and down with the waves, though poets would find this description much too prosaic. Mehmet Tevfik (1843–1893), for example, wrote: "You melancholy, wistful shores! Your quiet, silently fanning winds! Are they, as the sweetness of life, as calmness for the conscience and as a paradise of man, not the most worthy of description?"

the Byzantine Yoros Castle dominating the northern end of the village, which provides a spectacular view over the Bosphorus. The romantic setting is often used for wedding ceremonies. The ancient wooden houses in the Islamağa Sokağı that line the waterfront are well worth seeing on the way.

THE OTHER SIDE OF THE BOSPHORUS:
THE ASIAN PART OF THE CITY

The town of Beylerbeyı lies at the base of the First Bosphorus Bridge, on the less populous, more authentic Asian side, opposite the European neighborhood of Ortaköy. Here too, restaurants and cafés are clustered around the piers, while the sights include a picturesque little mosque with two slender minarets, and some traditional wooden villas by the water. The main attraction, however, is the similarly waterside Beylerbeyı Palace: a jewel of Ottoman palace architecture which, based on its façade and interior décor, rivals the much larger, and generally much more popular Dolmabahçe

The ferry terminal at Beylerbeyı and the nearby mosque (right and above) teem with life. The Beylerbeyı Palace (top) – built between 1860 and 1865 for foreign guests of state on the orders of Sultan Abdülaziz I – was once frequented by the most illustrious of visitors, including Britain's King Edward VIII, Austria's Emperor Franz Joseph and France's Empress Eugénie.

Palace on the European side. The similarity is actually no co-incidence; the palace was designed by Sarkis Bey Balyan (1835–1899), whose father built the Dolmabahçe Palace. Beylerbeyı served as a residence for visiting royalty, and many foreign kings, shahs and princesses have stayed here.

THE OTHER SIDE OF THE BOSPHORUS:
THE ASIAN PART OF THE CITY

Greeks founded the two settlements of Chalcedon and Chrysopolis here on the Asian side of the Bosphorus as early as the seventh century BC – ancient predecessors of the present-day Istanbul district of Üsküdar, which provides what is probably the most stunning view of the historic Old Town situated directly opposite in the west, and its southerly neighbor Kadıköy. Perched on a hillside ledge across from the pier in Üsküdar is the Mihrimah Mosque, also known as the "Iskele Mosque" because of its proximity to the dock (Turkish: *iskele*). Its construction, completed in 1548, was commis-

sioned by Sultan Süleyman I in honor of his daughter Mihrimah, the wife of Grand Vizier Rüstem Paşa. One particular architectural feature of the building designed by Sinan is the fact that the central main dome is only surrounded by three (one large and two smaller) half-domes.

Only dim light filters through the windows in the tambour and wall of the mosque (left and above), situated on the riverbank opposite the Topkapı Palace. Top: It was purely at the insistence of the people that a second minaret was added – something only reserved for sultans' mosques at the time – in order to allow strings of lights (*mahyâsi*) to be hung between them, as was the popular fashion in the 16th century.

THE OTHER SIDE OF THE BOSPHORUS: THE ASIAN PART OF THE CITY

Soaring up on a small island in the Bosphorus Strait, just 200 m (656 ft) off the Asian coast, is the Kız Kulesi Tower, erected in its present-day form in the 18th century. Home to a customs office as early as the fifth century BC, the tower itself was variously used as a prison. For James Bond (in *The World is Not Enough*, 1999), it was somewhere to save the world; for everyone else, the tower and the island is at least somewhere to spend an enjoyable day. Or an enjoyable evening, for the café (open during the day) and the chic restaurant and bar (open at night) both offer unparalleled views. Then

Formerly also known as "Leander's Tower", after the Greek myth of Hero and Leander, although this is set on the Dardanelles. The Turkish name Kız Kulesi, meaning "Maiden's Tower", relates to the legend of a princess who, according to a prophecy, would die of a snake bite. She was thus hidden here, but was still unable to escape her fate – the snake lay concealed in a fruit basket.

it's just a question of being lucky enough to have the moon high in the sky, while the stars twinkle and you yourself sit above the waves of the Bosphorus, in order to personally experience how the silvery light gives the historic Old Town a magical aura. The bar at the top has the best views.

Revolution creeps up on silent soles. It gives a subtle smile and has a name: here it is Zeynep Fadillioğlu. The opening of the Şakirin Mosque in Üsküdar in spring 2009 caused a minor sensation: the media headlines reported of "the first mosque designed by a woman", and it was declared with evident satisfaction that "a male bastion had fallen". However, Zeynep Fadillioğlu herself, an art historian and interior designer born in Istanbul in 1955, emphasizes the fact that "her" mosque was designed by the architect Hüsrev Tayla, who drew up the main plan for the religious building financed by

the wealthy Sakir family. Fadillioğlu, who made her name designing luxury hotels, was responsible for the interior design – which alone makes her a pioneer. And she also made a few radical changes compared to traditional Ottoman mosques, some of which even could be considered revolutionary.

"We opened up the façades and fitted filigree metal structures instead of walls", says the celebrated interior designer Zeynep Fadillioğlu. The mosque has an open-plan design in general, and men and women enter through the same entrance; they both have equal rights inside. "I thought there had to be boundaries", Fadillioğlu marvels, "But there aren't any. The limitations only exist in the mind."

THE OTHER SIDE OF THE BOSPHORUS: THE ASIAN PART OF THE CITY

The Haydarpaşa terminus station, built by German architects Otto Ritter and Helmut Cuno between 1906 and 1908, looms into view north of the port of Kadiköy. It is a three-winged complex with rounded turrets, arched entrances and an almost endless line of windows, making it appear more like a palace than a train station. The place from which suburban railways and trains today carry passengers to cities in eastern Turkey, like Ankara and Konya, once marked the start of much longer journeys: to Baghdad. German Emperor Wilhelm II (1859–1941) was responsible for developing and

The station building, magnificently adorned with sandstone reliefs and marble, looks like something out of *One Thousand and One Nights*. Supported by 220 wooden beams, it is best viewed from the water. Unfortunately, the roof structure and the upper levels were largely destroyed by a fire in 2010.

extending the section of what was then also known as the "Baghdad Railway", successfully gaining influence in a region dominated by the British and the French at the time. The railway was also very popular among Orient Express passengers, who were able to continue their journey here.

Writer Emine Sevgi Özdamar, born in the Turkish town of Malatya in 1946, once said that people in Istanbul don't know whether the sea cradles the city or the city cradles the sea. As a child, she was convinced that the sea was a woman, because it gave the people fish. But sometimes, when the south-westerly wind seized the ships, it became a man: "On those days, it was said that the sea was a sultan who stopped at no one and nothing." But when the wind is still and the sky a rich blue, when the summer heat creates a glistening sheen of dust and dirt over the cacophonous city, that's when it's time to head out to sea to the Princes' Islands, located some 20 km (12 miles) south of Istanbul, also known as Red Islands (Kızıl Adalar) or just Adalar. There are nine islands in total, and they are named after the fact that the obstreperous sons of rulers were banished here in

Byzantine times. Commoners probably wouldn't want to be banished here either – and indeed Leon Trotsky was one unhappy exile – but the islands are perfect for spending a day by the sea. And on the return journey, you can form your own opinion of the relationship between the city and the sea.

The Princes' Islands are also known locally as Kızıl Adaları ("Red Islands") because of their ferrous reddish stone. Only the four larger islands are constantly inhabited: Büyükada (left and top), Burgazada, Heybeliada and Kınalıada. A monastery was founded on Heybeliada in the 9th century, and today houses a prominent theological seminary of the Ecumenical Patriarchate of Constantinople (above).

View over Istanbul by night. An unforgettable experience when combined with good food.

COMPACT ISTANBUL

No other metropolis in the world can claim to straddle two continents. Although the districts on the European side of Istanbul offer more tourist attractions, it is definitely worth making a detour – by ferry or over a bridge – to the Asian side of Istanbul. Tradition and modernity intermix on both sides of the Bosphorus Strait, and the city's magnificence and diversity can be encountered on almost every street corner – ranging from the motley collection of bazaars, elegant shopping streets and impressive mosque architecture to the Turkish baths, or *hamams*, where guests will be indulged.

Situated in Istanbul's Edirnekapi district, the Chora Church became famous for the superb 13th and 14th-century mosaics and frescoes that were uncovered there.

MUSEUMS, MUSIC, DRAMA

Mosaics Museum The cultural site on the grounds of the Great Palace presents excavated mosaics which have been magnificently restored to almost their original condition. The Byzantine mosaics depict hunting scenes, representations of everyday life, and scenes from ancient mythological stories. The mosaics are displayed under a protective canopy.
Arasta Çarşisi,
Tel +90 (0) 212 518 12 05,
Thu–Sun 9.00–17.00.

Museum of Calligraphy Manuscripts from various eras are displayed in a former Qur'anic school, where they are considered a form of art. Here you can admire calligraphic art on paper, as well as on stone and glass. The collection of writing tools is also well worth seeing. The museum allows visitors to browse through a major part of Islamic culture, including also samples of bookbinding, holy relics and miniatures.
Beyazit Meydani,
Tel +90 (0) 212 527 58 51,
Thu–Sat 9.00–17.00.

Roxelane Hamam The former bathhouse also known as the Haseki Hürrem Sultan Hamamı, situated between the Blue Mosque and the Hagia Sophia, is today home to a museum. The bath, commissioned by and named after the wife of Sultan Süleyman I the Magnificent, is considered to be the finest example of architecture in Istanbul because of its virtually perfect symmetry. Mosaics and marble marquetry create a feeling of grandeur appreciated by the city's well-to-do citizens.
Ayasofya Meydani,
Tel +90 (0) 212 638 00 35,
Wed–Mon 9.00–17.00.

Vakıflar Carpet Museum This museum, situated on the grounds of the Blue Mosque, makes Oriental dreams come true. The artistically handmade carpets come from all over Turkey but especially from the region of Anatolia, and many are several centuries old. Although the carpets are presented in display cabinets with tinted glass to protect them from daylight, their full splendor can still be appreciated.
Imperial Pavilion,
Tel +90 (0) 212 518 87 54,
Thu–Sat 9.00–12.00,
13.00–16.00.

Chora Church Originally a Christian church, it was converted into a mosque under Ottoman rule in the 16th century, before ultimately being turned into a museum in 1948. Today it is home to some of the oldest and most magnificent mosaics from Byzantine times.

The show at the Dolphinarium is a spectacle not to be missed by any visitor, young or old.

Unlike many strictly stylized sculptures from that era, those displayed in this church are distinguished by extreme lightness and extensive detail. The same is true for the frescos, whose quality equals that of the mosaics.
Kariye Camii Sokak 6,
Tel +90 (0) 212 534 84 14,
Thu–Tue 9.00–16.30.

FESTIVALS AND EVENTS

Istanbul International Music Festival Symphony and chamber orchestras, operas and ballet performances, choral shows and jazz concerts form the essence of this annual festival, with the traditional highlight being Mozart's comical opera *The Abduction from the Seraglio*, for which the Topkapı Palace provides an appropriate historic setting.
www.iksv.org/muzik,
4 weeks in June.

Istanbul International Jazz Festival George Benson, Chick Corea and Dizzy Gillespie are just a few of the many world-famous musicians who have performed at this festival since it began in 1994, and who have justified Istanbul's reputation as one of the major European centers for this type of music. Concerts are held at several different venues, for example the Topkapı Palace and on the grounds of the Archaeological Museum.
www.iksv.org/caz,
2 weeks in July.

Istanbul Biennal The city on the Bosphorus becomes the main focus of the international art scene during this festival, held every odd-numbered year since 1987. Along with the Biennials in Venice, São Paulo and Sydney, it has established itself as one of the leading events of its kind. Excitement and suspense are generated by the contrast between contemporary art and the historic ambiance exuded by illustrious venues such as the Hagia Eirene Church in the Old Town.
Tel +90 (0) 212 334 07 00,
www.iksv.org/bienal,
2 months in autumn.

SPORT, GAMES, FUN

Bosphorus cruise An insider's tip for anyone wanting to get away from the hustle and bustle of the large metropolis for a while: ferry boats journey up the Bosphorus toward the Black Sea, a trip lasting several hours and departing daily from the ferry port of Eminönü. Food is available onboard. You can leave the ship at one of the piers and have a look around one of Istanbul's quieter districts – or simply enjoy the ride on the water.
Eminönü ferry terminal.

Çemberlitaş Hamam – a large number of spa treatments are offered in an Oriental ambience.

Old Town tour The many architectural and art-historic attractions of Istanbul's Old Town are best experienced as part of a private tour – small, with first-hand information. A local English-speaking guide will show you the most important sights. The length and route of the tours through the Old Town can be "off the peg" or tailored to the individual customers' requirements.
Prof Kazim Gurkan
Caddesi 34,
Tel +90 (0) 212 543 43 36,
www.istanbulguide.de

The scent of the Orient The Spice Bazaar (Egyptian Bazaar) is not only a stunning spectacle to behold, but also brings together a number of fragrances and aromas associated with the Orient. Whether it be thyme or saffron, peppermint or sage, ginger or pepper, cinnamon or cumin, cloves or coriander – you might want to simply saunter through the bazaar with your eyes firmly shut and be guided purely by your sense of smell.

Dolphinarium Comprising seven large pools, the Dolphinarium, was established in 2008. The most spectacular shows are held in the main pool, which has a radius of 16.5 m (54 ft) and is 5 m (15 ft) deep. Just under 1,000 visitors can attend the approximately one-hour shows at a time. After undergoing a briefing, visitors can additionally swim with the dolphins and have their photograph taken. There are also white whales, walruses and Northern fur seals. The Dolphinarium also has a café.
Silahtara Caddesi 2/4,
Tel +90 (0) 212 581 78 78,
www.istanbuldolphinarium.
com, Wed, Thu 11.00, 13.30,
Fri 11.00, Sat, Sun 14.00, 17.00.

Haggling The prices quoted by dealers, particularly at the bazaars – such as the Grand Bazaar – should not be taken as fixed prices, and can often be significantly reduced through skilful negotiation. The quoted prices usually include a certain degree of "leeway", which applies for items such as clothing, fabrics, leather goods, jewelry, carpets and souvenirs. Particularly when it comes to more expensive items, you should also always check before buying whether these are originals or just cheap imitations.

HEALTH & BEAUTY

Cagaloglu Hamam This wellness oasis with its many steam baths and treatments is open to men and women at different times. The hamam is one of the grandest and most illustrious bathhouses in Istanbul, and the staff cater excellently for

Books on Turkey, whether its history, art, literature or religion – you're guaranteed to find them all at the Galeri Kayseri.

all visitors. The complex's history dates back almost 300 years, and it has welcomed numerous famous guests.
Cagagoglu Hamami, Sokak 34,
Tel +90 (0) 212 522 24 24,
www.cagaloghamami.com.tr
8.00–20.00 (for women),
8.00–22.00 (for men).

Süleymaniye Hamam Sultan Süleyman I the Magnificent had the bathhouse built in the mid-16th century as part of the Sultan Süleyman Mosque which also bears his name. The grandeur of its exquisite interior décor is enhanced by the amazing marble work. Today, guests can still enjoy the full treatment of a Turkish steam bath, wash and massage. A unisex hamam, it caters very well for foreign visitors.
Mimar Sinan Caddesi 20,
Tel +90 (0) 212 519 55 69,
www.suleymaniyehamami.
com.tr, 10.00–24.00 daily.

Çemberlitaş Hamam Various reflex-zone massages and aromatherapy treatments are popular additions to the conventional range of health and beauty treatments available to guests at a typical Turkish hamam. Many guests also love the other special features such as face and neck treatments using natural mud.
Vezirhan Caddesi 8,
Tel +90 (0) 212 522 79 74,
www.cemberlitashamami.
com.tr, 6.00–24.00 daily.

SHOPPING

Muhlis Günbatti If you are looking for the perfect carpet you may get lucky here. One of the most famous shops in the Grand Bazaar, it also sells tapestries and wall hangings, bedspreads, textiles such as Ottoman kaftans, and an exquisite selection of the finest materials, fabrics and silks.

Many carpets and fabrics have Central Asian patterns with floral elements.
Perdahçilar Sokak 48,
Tel +90 (0) 212 511 65 62,
Mon–Sat 9.00–20.00.

Galeri Şirvan The number of carpet dealers in the Grand Bazaar is daunting. But there are big differences when it comes to the quality of the items. This shop, which sells handmade *kelims* crafted by ethnic groups in Anatolia, is a good place to check out.
Keseciler Caddesi 55,
Tel +90 (0) 212 520 62 24,
Mon–Sat 9.00–20.00.

Galeri Kayseri This well laid-out bookshop sells English-language literature on all sorts of subjects relating to Turkey – including history, art, architecture, archaeology, religion, literature from various eras, cooking and traveling. Galeri

Şişko Osman sells magnificent, top-quality carpets.

Kayseri is the most famous bookshop of its kind in all of Turkey, and its academics and experts are constantly expanding its amazing collection of well over 2,000 Turkish interest titles. It also has an impressive selection of Turkish folklore music on CD.
Divanyolu Caddesi 58,
Tel +90 (0) 212 516 33 66,
www.galerikayseri.com,
Mon–Sat 9.00–20.00.

Şişko Osman This is one of the best places to visit for high-quality carpets at (usually) fair prices, although these have to be negotiated. Some connoisseurs say no other dealer in Istanbul knows carpets like Şişko Osman. The service offered by the family business, now in its fourth generation, is flawless: the carpets are also sent to the customer's home address, and the website provides extensive information about all things

carpet-related. According to Şişko Osman, "it is not enough to know about the rug but you have to read it".
Kapalıçarşı Zincirli Han 15,
Tel +90 (0) 212 528 35 48,
www.siskoosman.com,
Mon–Sat 8.30–19.00.

Cocoon Located in the historic Arasta Bazaar, in the shadows of the Blue Mosque, this shop is filled with the magical atmosphere of a Thousand and One Nights. Apart from carpets and blankets from Central Asian countries, Iran and Anatolia, it also sells clothing from other Arab nations such as Yemen and Syria. Many international stars in the Middle Eastern show business world wear coats, jackets and hats from Cocoon, whose selection additionally includes handbags, belts and jewelry. The store has several other outlets and carpet galleries in Istanbul.

Küçük Ayasofya Caddesi 13,
Tel +90 (0) 212 638 62 71,
www.cocoontr.com

Efe Jewelry This specialized store sells beautiful, finely crafted gold and silver jewelry in all shapes and forms, from wedding bands and bangles to children's jewelry, religious art, cufflinks and tie clips. Unlike many market stalls, the items are not replicas, but originals. Efe Jewelry typifies the highest quality Turkish craftsmanship.
Nuruosmaniye Caddesi 41,
9.00–21.00 daily.

Sivasli Yazmaci This shop in the Grand Bazaar sells casual clothing, as well as more select items such as beautiful hand-embroidered or even crocheted blankets. Sivasli Yazmaci is also a veritable treasure chest for fine cotton fabrics in every color. A large part of the range comes from eastern Anatolia.

Sarniç Lokantasi – Turkish specialties are served in atmospheric vaulted rooms.

Yaglikçilar Sokak 57,
Tel +90 (0) 212 526 77 48,
8.30–19.00 daily.

Ethnicon The concept is really quite simple: fabrics left over from carpets, curtains and other items are used to make "new" *kelims* based on the patchwork principle, fusing contemporary and various ethnic styles. The result is unusual, but has enabled Ethnicon to make a name for itself, even beyond Istanbul's borders. And: every item is unique.
Kapalicarsi Takkeciler
Sokak 58–60,
Tel +90 (0) 212 527 68 41,
www.ethnicon.com,
Mon–Sat 8.30–19.00.

EATING AND DRINKING

Rami This museum-restaurant was named after Turkish painter Rami Uluer, and is decorated with some pictures of the impressionist artist. Classical music creates an almost festive atmosphere, and patrons are served traditional Turkish cuisine of the highest quality. The ingredients come from all over the country. From the terrace diners can enjoy a superb view of the Blue Mosque.
Utangaç Sokak 6,
Tel +90 (0) 212 517 65 93,
www.ramirestaurant.com

Arcadia The view from the rooftop terrace of the restaurant of the hotel bearing the same name could not be more spectacular – the finest buildings in the Old Town virtually lie right at the patrons' feet. Apart from Turkish dishes, the menu also covers cuisine from other Mediterranean regions, including a large selection of fish and seafood.
Dr Imran Oktem Caddesi 1,
Tel +90 (0) 212 516 96 96,
www.hotelarcadiaistanbul.com

Balikçi Sabahattin The seafood restaurant which has been running since 1927 has long been one of Istanbul's most reputable eating establishments, serving consistently good food. The desserts are sweet seduction at its best. Al fresco dining is available in fine weather.
Seyit Hasan Sokak 50,
Tel +90 (0) 212 458 18 24,
www.balikcisabahattin.com

Sarniç Lokantasi Soft lighting from chandeliers, vaulted ceilings and mirrors create an atmosphere that is perfect for a romantic candlelight dinner. The chefs indulge guests with superb meat and fish dishes, using the freshest of ingredients, as well as vegetarian options. Book early!
Soguçeflme Sokak,
Tel +90 (0) 212 512 42 91,
www.sarnicrestaurant.com,
19.00–24.00 daily.

COMPACT ISTANBUL

Contemporary Turkish art is on display at the Istanbul Modern.

MUSEUMS, MUSIC, DRAMA

Ottoman Bank Museum This exhibition is housed in the former headquarters of the Ottoman Bank which operated as the central bank, bank of issue, and treasurer of the Ottoman Empire. It showcases not only documents on the history of banking since the mid-19th century, but also explores social history since that time. The objects displayed – banknotes, coins, photos, contracts – provide an excellent chronological overview of the last decades of the Ottoman Empire and early years of the republic.
Voyvoda Caddesi 35–37,
Tel +90 (0) 212 292 76 05,
www.obmuseum.com,
10.00–18.00 daily.

Istanbul Modern The Istanbul Museum of Modern Art was opened in a former warehouse right on the Golden Horn in 2004, and it was Turkey's first private museum for modern art at the time. Paintings, including watercolors and landscapes, sculptures and photographs are displayed over two levels. The objects are created predominantly by Turkish artists, and provide a good overview of the evolution of modern and contemporary Turkish art from the earliest to the present day.
Meclis-i Mebusan
Caddesi 35–37,
Tel +90 (0) 212 334 73 00,
www.istanbulmodern.org,
Tue–Sat 10.00–18.00
(Thu until 20.00).

Maritime Museum This museum, founded in 1961, details the history and development of Turkish seafaring since the start of the Ottoman Empire. The exhibits include nautical charts from various eras, model ships, navigation instruments, weaponry and portraits of famous captains. Some rowboats that were once used by the sultans to cross the Bosphorus can also be seen.
Hayrettin Paşa Iskelesi Sokak,
Tel +90 (0) 212 327 43 45,
Wed–Sun 9.00–17.00.

Dolmabahçe Palace The palace on the European side of the Bosphorus was opened in 1856 and served – with a brief interruption – as the sultan's residence until 1922. Exceptionally lavishly appointed throughout, the extravagant use of gold, Egyptian marble and glass is particularly impressive. Guided tours take visitors to the sultan's private quarters as well as the public areas, including the reception rooms and majestic ceremonial hall.
Dolmabahçe Caddesi,
Tel +90 (0) 212 236 90 00,
www.dolmabahcepalace.com,
Tue, Wed, Fri–Sun
9.00–16.00.

Alongside historic exhibits, you can also admire valuable Qur'anic calligraphies at the Sakıp Sabancı Museum.

Museum of Fine Arts Some 2,500 paintings and 400 sculptures dating from the 19th and 20th centuries are housed in this museum, opened in 1937 in the crown prince's suites of Dolmabahçe Palace. It includes works by Turkish artists (for example, Osman Hamdi and Hoca Ali Riza), many of which portray Istanbul's Oriental traditions. Some pieces by well-known Western European painters (including Pablo Picasso and Henri Matisse) are also on display here.
Hayrettin Paşa Iskelesi Sokak,
Tel +90 (0) 212 261 42 98,
Wed–Sun 12.00–16.00.

Rahmi Koç Museum Science and technology are the main focus of these interesting permanent exhibits, with topics ranging from transport, to communication and technical devices. Some parts of the aviation, shipping and railway sections are outdoors. Children will love the interactive games.
Hasköy Caddesi 5,
Tel +90 (0) 212 369 66 00,
www.rmk-museum.org.tr,
Apr–Sep Tue–Fri 10.00–17.00,
Sat, Sun 10.00–20.00,
Oct–Mar Tue–Fri 10.00–17.00,
Sat, Sun 10.00–18.00.

Sakıp Sabancı Museum A wide range of art forms are shown in one of the Sabancı family's fine urban villas. The Qur'anic manuscripts, sculptures from the Byzantine and Ottoman Empires, furniture and other handicrafts from the 18th and 19th centuries, as well as paintings by Turkish artists from the mid-19th century, are among the items on display.
Sakıp Sabancı Caddesi 42,
Tel +90 (0) 212 277 22 00,
www.sabanciuniv.edu,
Tue, Thu, Fri–Sun
10.00–18.00, Wed
10.00–20.00

Aşiyan Museum The name of the museum has nothing to do with Asia, and instead means "bird's nest" in translation. It was once the home of one of Turkey's best-known writers, Tevfik Fikret (1867–1915), whose many fans included the man who would later become the father of the Turkish Republic, Kemal Atatürk. Fikret's personal belongings are on display, as are some paintings around his works.
Aşiyan Yolu,
Tel +90 (0) 212 263 69 6,
Tue, Wed, Fri–Sun 9.00–17.00.

Mevlevi Loge The museum is housed in a monastery and dedicated to the Dervish Order to which the friars once belonged. Visitors can view the dancing hall (18th century), where the whirling dances, also known as Sufi whirling, are still performed on the last Sunday afternoon of each

COMPACT ISTANBUL

Whirling Dervishes at the Yildiz Palace, which served as the residence of the sultans and their court until the late 19th century.

month. Musical instruments, documents and photographs are displayed.
Galipdede Caddesi 15,
Tel +90 (0) 212 245 41 41,
Wed–Mon 9.00–16.00.

Military Museum A museum and concert hall under one roof: Turkey's one-thousand-year military history is told using striking pieces of battle equipment such as curved daggers, helmets and ornamentally adorned shields. Generals' encampment tents in which the battles were planned and prepared can also be viewed. The military museum is additionally used as a venue for concerts put on by the Mehter military band whose origins date back to the 14th century and the Janissaries. The music also incorporates classical elements.
Valikona i Caddesi 42,
Tel +90 (0) 212 233 27 20,
Wed–Sun 9.00–17.00.

Yildiz Palace The walled palace situated in Yildiz Park comprises a complex of buildings dating back to the 19th and 20th centuries. The property includes the Yildiz Theater and Opera House, built in 1889 and which is today home to a museum. The former carpentry workshop now also houses a museum. The interior, with its vivid color scheme of bright blues and golds, is topped with a star-studded domed ceiling, playing on the palace's name (*yildiz* meaning "star").
Çira an Caddesi 42,
Tel +90 (0) 212 258 30 80,
Wed–Sun 9.30–16.00.

Yeni Melek Show Theater Anyone wanting to see Turkish music stars perform live has the best chance of doing so here at the former cinema and three-tier music venue. The illustrious repertoire ranges from pop to classical music, to theater and video art, to many other genres of visual arts, and the performances are put on by both renowned artists and talented newcomers.
Gazeteci Erol Dernek Sokak 13,
Tel +90 (0) 212 236 68 54.

Atatürk Cultural Center Istanbul's largest art and music venue (Atatürk Kültür Merkezi or AKM) for cultural events is home to prestigious ensembles such as the Turkish State Opera and Ballet, while its smaller galleries occasionally host art exhibitions. A rather brutalist building, it burned down in 1970 during a performance and was rebuilt. After further extensive renovations, the center was given an elegant new look in early 2010, to mark Istanbul's year as the European Capital of Culture.
Taksim Meydani,
Tel +90 (0) 212 251 56 00.

Magnificent tulips on parade in the Emirgan Park, an unparalleled feast for the eyes.

Akbank Sanat Cultural Center In addition to the prestigious exhibits of paintings and sculptures from various epochs, the concerts held at this contemporary art center are particular popular, ranging from classical music to jazz. The center also hosts the Akbank Jazz Festival, the Akbank Short Film Festival, and the Zeynep Tanbay Dance Project in its dance hall.
Istiklal Caddesi 16,
Tel +90 (0) 212 252 35 00.

Cemal Reşit Rey Concert Hall The concert hall named after the famous Turkish opera composer Cemal Reşit Rey (1904–1985) is one of the most prominent venues in Istanbul and originally built for classical music performances. Today it presents predominantly Turkish folklore and classical music, although it also regularly hosts a variety of music festivals – from baroque to piano music.

Darülbedayi Caddesi 16,
Tel +90 (0) 212 231 54 97,
www.ccrks.org

FESTIVALS AND EVENTS

Tulip Festival The tulip gardens in Emirgan Park vibrantly burst into full bloom every year in April. The festival commemorates the time when the sultans would decorate their prestigious palace gardens with thousands of tulips, and the city planted three million tulips in celebration. Apart from the overwhelming display of color, it is the artistic arrangements which are impressive.
Emirgan Sahil Yolu,
several weeks in Apr.

Efes Pilsen Blues Festival The music festival sponsored by, and named after, a Turkish brewery attracts blues fans from all over Turkey. The artists include renowned blues greats

from Europe and North America. The festival is held at several different venues.
1 weekend early Nov.

Mevlana Festival A lavish party is held in the Mevlevi Lodge in honor of Mevlana, the 13th-century mystic, writer and founder of the famous Order of the Whirling Dervishes. Spectacular whirling dances are the main highlight, transporting visitors back several centuries.
Galipdede Caddesi 15,
1 week in Dec.

SPORT, GAMES, FUN

Miniatürk A visit to the world of miniatures on the banks of the Golden Horn is fun for all the family. This theme park, opened in 2003 and spread over 6 ha (15 acres), is home to more than one hundred miniatures of prominent attractions in Istanbul and other Turkish

Numerous restaurants and bars provide sustenance and refreshments on SuAda Island.

cities as well as former Ottoman Empire sites that are now outside Turkey – from the Hagia Sophia to the Topkapı Palace, from the Galata Tower to the city's airport, from the Temple of Artemis in Ephesus to the Mausoleum at Halicarnassus. It also has a museum celebrating the life of Atatürk.
Imrahor Caddesi,
Tel +90 (0) 212 222 28 82,
www.miniaturk.com.tr,
9.00–17.00 daily.

Football Istanbul is undoubtedly the home of football in Turkey, and Turkey is one of the most ardent football nations in the world. The stadiums are notorious for their often heated atmosphere, but for many fans, a visit to these cauldrons of pandemonium is one of life's experiences. In Istanbul, the traditional "big three" clubs, Galatasaray, Beşiktaş and Fenerbahçe, all compete

with one another, recruiting international stars from Europe and South America. Of course, the atmosphere at the derbies, when two Istanbul clubs face off, is incomparably electric.
www.galatasaray.org,
www.bjk.com.tr,
www.fenerbahce.org

Ride on the Tünel railway The underground railway, which started operating in 1875, is the world's oldest funicular railway. It connects the districts of Karaköy and Beyoglu, involving an almost 62 m (203 ft) difference in elevation over a distance of just 606 m (1,988 ft). The ride is nostalgic, and also saves you making the exhausting climb by foot.
Stationen Karaköy
and Beyo lu.

Pool party on SuAda A man-made island in the Bosphorus, situated around 150 m (492 ft)

off the coast, is used as a party location, complete with its own swimming pool – turquoise in color, of course. Here, virtually between Europe and Asia, you can relax, take a dip, and enjoy the view of the city skyline or passing ships from the poolside. There are several bars and restaurants available too. SuAda Island can be reached on one of the free boats regularly sailing there.
Ferry pier Kuruçeşme,
www.suada.com.tr

Cooking classes Whether you are a fan of Turkish cuisine for its healthy and delicious hearty food, or whether your leanings are more for tempting sweets, a three-week course at the Chef's Cooking School in Istanbul offers pure culinary pleasure. Under expert instruction, you learn to prepare your own *boreks* (stuffed pastries), *zeytinyaglis* (vegetables dishes),

The Dutch singer Tineke Postma guests at the Jazzclub Nard.

Meşrutiyet Caddesi 145,
Tel +90 (0) 212 245 58 10,
13.00–4.00 daily.

Baykus Locals and tourists all feel at home in this bar. You can have a meal here or just pop in to enjoy a drink, and either start or finish your evening out here. The meals and the cocktails are both top class, and the service is pleasantly speedy.
Bekar Sokak 22,
Tel +90 (0) 212 292 88 44,
Wed, Thu 21.30–2.00,
Fri, Sat 22.00–3.00.

Blackk As the name suggests, black is the theme that dominates here. Whether floors, screens, tables or the staff uniforms – all is black. The fashionably dressed clientele, often including stars and starlets, meanwhile introduce a splash of color. Blackk comprises a (calmer) resto-lounge as well as a club that's one of the

trendiest in town. A disco ball hangs above the dancefloor.
Muallim Naci Caddesi 71,
Tel +90 (0) 212 236 72 56,
www.blackk.net,
22.00–4.00 daily.

The Hall In the Beyoglu district, famous for its nightlife, this is one of the hottest of all places. Live bands and DJs get the audience going at the weekend until 4.00 in the morning. A visit to The Hall is also a great plan for nightowls that have long outgrown their teenage years or their twenties. And it doesn't matter a bit that the drinks are somewhat more expensive here.
Küçük Bayram Sokak 7,
Tel +90 (0) 212 244 87 36,
www.thehall.com.tr

Anjelique This exclusive night spot in a first-class location on the Bosphorus attracts a young and stylish crowd. The Anjelique

has a bar and a restaurant, and form the latter's terrace you can enjoy outstanding views of the Asian side of Istanbul. At night, especially in the summer months, the terrace turns into a dancefloor, where you can dance the night away under the starry skies.
Muallim Naci Caddesi 5,
Tel +90 (0) 212 327 28 44,
www.blackk.net,
May–Oct 18.00–4.00 daily.

Nardis Many greats from the world of jazz regularly appear at this legendary club not far from the Galata Tower. As well as Turkish musicians, soloists and bands from other countries also perform here from time to time. You are well-advised to reserve your tickets early. The club also boasts its own restaurant.
Kuledibi Sokak 14,
Tel + 90 (0) 212 244 63 27,
www.nardisjazz.com

A view of the magnificent auditorium of Süreyya, the spectacular Istanbul Opera House

MUSEUMS, MUSIC, DRAMA

Oyuncak Museum Although this museum is dedicated to toys it is of interest not only to children – all those who stayed young at heart will enjoy this trip down memory lane and love its model train sets, model cars and Anatolian shadow puppets. You can also admire here tin soldiers, music boxes, teddy bears and porcelain dolls in large numbers.
Ömerpaşa Caddesi;
Dr. Zeki Zeren Sokak 17,
Tel +90 (0) 216 359 45 50,
www.istanbuloyuncak
muzesi.com,
Tue–Sun 9.30–18.00.

Istanbul Grafik Sanatlar-Museum Known also under its English name of IMOGA (Istanbul Museum of Graphic Art) this museum exhibits around 1,200 works by more than 80 artists on six floors, making it one of the largest art museums in the entire country. Of particular interest is the department devoted to stencil printing and lithography.
Ünahan Mahallesi
Keban Caddesi 20,
Tel +90 (0) 216 470 92 92,
www.imoga.org,
Tue–Sun 9.30–18.00.

Florence Nightingale Museum An unusual location for a cultural center: this museum, established in honor of the famous British nurse Florence Nightingale (1820–1910) is housed in the Selimiye Barracks. Particularly during the Krimean war, Florence Nightingale campaigned tirelessly for better medical care and provisions for the injured soldiers. On show here are medals, photographs, the sultan's presents as well as the famous lamp that earned her the epithet "Lady with the Lamp".

Çeşme-i Kebir Caddesi,
Tel +90 (0) 216 556 80 80,
Sat, Sun 9.00–17.00.

Süreyya The Istanbul Opera House is at home in an Art Deco building dating from 1927. Aside from pera and classical concerts it also stages ballet and drama performances. The auditorium, furnished in red, offers seating for 570 spectators and since extensive renovation work has boasted of the most advanced lighting and sound technology available.
Bahariye Caddesi Caferağ
a Mahallesi 29,
Tel +90 (0) 216 346 15 31,
www.sureyyaoperasi.org

Mydonose Showland This venue, famous for staging well-loved musicals (Grease, for example), popular festivals and other musical events, has first-class stage acts throughout the year. Around two-thirds

The entrance are of the Oyun Atölyesi Sahnesi Theater which stages European classics

of the complex, measuring some 24,000 sq m (258,240 sq ft) overall, are in the open air, the rest is covered.
Dünya Ticaret Merkezi Yani, Tel +90 (0) 212 345 05 80.

Oyun Atölyesi Sahnesi All the great classics are performed here. The varied program includes everything from Euripides and Molière to Shakespeare, plus modern pieces – all in Turkish of course.
Dr. Esat Işik Caddesi 3, Tel +90 (0) 216 349 98 78, www.oyunatolyesi.com

FESTIVALS AND EVENTS

International Istanbul Theater Festival Turkish versions of Western European plays are performed by some theaters in Istanbul, for example by the Caddebostan Cultural Center, the HaldunTaner, the Sabanci University Performance Centre and the Üsküdar Tekel on the Asian side of the city.
www.iksv.org/tiyatro, mid–May to mid–Jun.

SPORT, GAMES, FUN

Formula 1™ Races Since 2005, the Formula 1™ Races have been one the highlights in Istanbul's sports calendar. They take place on the Istanbul Park Circuit in the Tuzla district. Every year on a weekend in August, around 125,000 fans of the motorsport descend on the area for this event. In summer, the racing circuit is also used for staging the world championships and motorbike and touring car races.
Göçbeyli Köyü Yolu, Tel +90 (0) 216 446 83 73, www.istanbulparkcircuit.com

Cruise to the Princes' Islands It takes less than an hour to get from the ferry pier in Kadiköy to the Princes' Islands in the Sea of Marmara. An excursion here will be in sharp contract to the hectic city life in Istanbul and promises a few hours of rest and relaxation. The islands are ideally suited for strolls among the green spaces and the sublime villas of well-to-do Istanbul residents. On some of the islands you can also take a ride in a horse-drawn carriage.
Ferry pier Kadiköy.

Dodo Sea Club The city on the Bosphorus also boasts some beach resorts, all equipped to the highest standards and making for excellent swimming fun. From the shores on the Asian side you can also enjoy superb views of the skyline on the European side while enjoying a swim. When you're in the water, you should always be aware, however, of possible strong currents. There's also a beach bar and a kiosk.

Istanbul's International Dance Festival has a multifaceted range of dance forms of the highest order in its repertory.

Ankara Mercan
Cinarli Sokak 1,
Tel +90 (0) 216 446 83 73,
www.istanbulbeach.com/
dodo-sea-club

Bosphorus Zoo A visit to this animal park outside the city gates promises great fun for young and old alike. Established in 1990, the zoo provides an overview of the fauna in the transitional zone between Europe and Asia. Bird species are particularly well represented, and in the "Bird Paradise" you can experience a cross-section of birdlife on all continents. A botanical garden is attached to the zoo.
Emtas Bogaziçi, Tuzla Caddesi
15, Bayramoglu-Darica,
Tel +90 (0) 262 653 66 66,
www.farukyalcinzoo.com,
9.00–17.00 daily.

Drive across the Bosphorus
The European side of the city especially boasts a rather breathtaking skyline, characterized by numerous slim minarets. Take a bus from the Asian side across the Bosphorus Bridge, Opened in 1973, it measures more than 1,500 m (4,922 ft) in length and you'll have plenty of time to admire the views of the city. As the road is 64 m (210 ft) above the sea you can even see far-away ships on the Bosphorus.

Istanbul Marathon Participants, who find the classic marathon distance of 42 km (26 miles) a bit too long may instead run shorter distances of 8 or 15 km (5 or 9 miles). These competitions are the only official such races anywhere in the world that take the runners into two continents. The race starts in Üsküdar on the Asian side of Istanbul, not far from the Bosphorus Bridge, which you run across right at the start of the race. The course then continues through several districts on the European side.

HEALTH & BEAUTY

Çinili Hamam – Üsküdar This hamam dating from the 17th century is one of the oldest in Istanbul and also one of only few Turkish bathhouses on the Asian side. The staff speak only little English but this does not affect the quality of their excellent treatments in any way.
Murat Reis Mahallesi
Cavusdere Caddesi,
Tel +90 (0) 216 334 97 10,
www.cinilihamam.8m.com,
7.00–22.00 daily (men),
8.00–18.00 daily (women).

SHOPPING

Bit Pazari There is nothing that you can't find on this flea-market. The goods on sale range from art and kitsch to

The greatest event in the annual sports calendar is the 43-km-long (26-mile) Istanbul Marathon right across the city, between Europe and Asia.

furnishings. If you're on the lookout for a mirror, an old (not too valuable) piece of furniture or a cheap Oriental carpet – this is where in all probability you'll find what you are after. *Büyük Hamam Sokak 30/32, Mon–Sat 8.00–19.00.*

EATING AND DRINKING

Il Piccolo This restaurant is one of the best-known eateries on the Asian side. On the menu, as well as Turkish cuisine, you'll also find dishes from the other Mediterranean countries, including a variety of meat dishes, and also excellent pizzas and pasta dishes. A good selection of wines. *Bagdat Caddesi, Ögün Sokak 2, Tel +90 (0) 216 369 64 43, 11.00–24.00 daily.*

Kizkulesi The Leander Tower is located on a small island, just off the coast at Üsküdar. Once used as a lighthouse, the tower has since been converted as a restaurant specializing in absolute gourmet food. Occasionally there is live music (predominantly Turkish folklore). On the upper floor a bar has been set up and from its terrace you can enjoy excellent panoramic views. The restaurant will arrange a transport service to take you here and back to your hotel. *Kizkulesi Salacak Mevkii Üsküdar, Tel +90 (0) 216 342 47 47, www.kizkulesi.com.tr, 20.00–24.00 daily.*

Hidiv Kasri Amidst greenery but still right by the Bosphorus you can enjoy your meal on the terrace of this restaurants situated on a slope. Choose among a good selection of dishes while marveling at the idyllic views. However, the indoor ambience in the dining room housed in a palace is also very pleasant. The menu's emphasis is on fish and seafood, but you can find all the other dishes here that make the Turkish cuisine so charming. *Hidiv Yolu 32, Tel +90 (0) 216 425 06 03, 9.00–24.00 daily.*

NIGHTLIFE

Kadiköy One oft he most popular nightlife districts on the Asian side is Kadiköy, with the Kadife Sokak street attracting the liveliest crowds of partygoers. The street is lined by countless bars and clubs which has earned it the name of "Bar Street" among locals. Particular hotspots are the Isis Bar (at No. 26) and the Karga Bar (at No. 16). Most of these establishments will not close until the late morning hours. *Kadife Sokak*

HOTELS

DREAM VILLA ON THE BOSPHORUS

A'JIA

This luxuriously appointed boutique hotel is housed in a magnificent, snow-white Ottoman villa. It wows its guests not only with its excellent location right on the Bosphorus, but also with its contemporary interior design. The sixteen rooms are individually furnished and all enjoy superb views of the sea. Guests at the award-winning hotel restaurant can indulge in a range of innovative Mediterranean dishes.

Ahmet Rasim Pafla Yalisi
Cubuklu Caddesi 27,
Tel +90 (0) 216 413 93 00,
www.ajiahotel.com

OLD TOWN AND EYÜP

Hotel Amira Functionality and hightech comfort are the trademarks of the Amira. Yet the rooms all boast a cozy atmosphere too, and feature fascinating details such as painted ceilings and designer coffee tables. The bathrooms are equipped with rainwater showers, some also have jacuzzis. The hotel is situated in the immediate vicinity of one of the most-visited attractions.
Kucuk Ayasofya Mah.
Mustafapasa Sokak 79,
Tel +90 (0) 212 516 16 40,
www.hotelamira.com

Celal Sultan Hotel The stylish rooms feature double glazing and are ideal refuges to chill out after a hectic day in the metropolis. The lobby is held in hues of red and features a bar – ideal for a drink or a coffee before you take your evening meal in the hotel's own Ata Restaurant, where the very finest of Turkish and Ottoman cuisine is on offer.
Yerebatan Caddesi
Salkimsogut Sokak 16,
Tel +90 (0) 212 520 93 23,
www.celalsultan.com

Hotel Empress Zoe The hotel, named after a Byzantine empress and comprising 12 townhouses, transports you into another world. There is a great love of detail everywhere, with wood, stone and Turkish textiles used generously in the room designs. Some guests find it so hard to part from the lushly planted garden, surrounded by ruins, that they postpone their visits of the city to the evening hours. A spiral staircase connects the two levels (there is no elevator).
Akbiyik Caddesi 4/1,
Tel +90 (0) 212 518 25 04,
www.emzoe.com

BEYOGLU/BEŞIKTAŞ/SARIYER

Sofa Hotel You can feel the special style here as soon as you enter the hotel lobby – works of art characterize the inspiring atmosphere in this house. The rooms offer a perfect mix of ultramodern comfort and a personalized ambience. The spa area, held in warm natural hues and which of course includes a hamam, exudes an Oriental feel. The hotel also benefits from its location close to shopping arcades, restaurants and art galleries. The Sofa Hotel is one of the preferred places to stay at for Turkish celebrities.
Tesvikiye Caddesi 41,
Tel +90 (0) 212 368 18 18,
www.thesofahotel.com

Bentley Hotel Interior designers from Milan are responsible for the furnishing of the rooms and the public spaces. THey

TIPS FOR SPECIAL HOTELS

The elegant Ottoman villa is a veritable eyecatcher on the Asian shores of the Bosphorus.

achieved a fusion of elements from East and West, creating an ultramodern hotel, which provides plenty of opportunity for guests to retreat. Among its residents are many business people who appreciate such tranquility. The restaurant provides international favorites – outstanding fusion cuisine of the very highest quality.
Halaskargazi Caddesi 75,
Tel +90 (0) 212 291 77 30,
www.bentley-hotel.com

Ansen 130 Suites This five-floor hotel was appointed with great care and attention to detail. The result is a harmonious blend of elegance and individuality. Each of the ten generously sized suites is furnished to a theme – they all feature large bathrooms and huge writing desks.
Mesrutiyet Caddesi 70,
Tel +90 (0) 212 248 88 08,
www.ansensuites.com

Hotel Sultania The Sultania is a bridge between the charme of long-gone times and hyper-modern comfort for all the most demanding guests. According to the house's motto, every guest should feel like a sultan here. Style elements from the era of the Ottoman Empire create a comfortable historic ambience. Each of the 42 rooms is named after a wife of one of the sultans, and features an oil painting with the portrait of the lade who gave her name.
Ebusuud Caddesi Mehmet Murat Sokak 4,
Tel +90 (0) 212 520 77 88,
www.hotelsultania.com

Midtown The photographs of Istanbul in the rooms and corridors will make you want to explore the city. The Midtown boasts of adhering to the highest environmental standards and it has been certified ac-

cordingly. The rooms are minimalist in their décor, but they leave no wish unfulfilled. The More Restaurant has award-winning chefs who present you with exciting variations on Turkish classics.
Lamartin Caddesi 13,
Tel +90 (0) 212 361 67 67,
www.midtown-hotel.com

ASIAN SIDE

Sumahan Housed in a 19th-century property, the Sumahan is still a family business today. Wood, marble, brick and luxurious fabrics create a warm atmosphere throughout. From the rooms and suites (some having their own hamam) you can watch the ships and ferries glide along the Bosphorus. Taking afternoon tea in the garden is another treat.
Kuleli Caddesi 51,
Tel +90 (0) 216 422 80 80,
www.sumahan.com

HOTELS

HISTORIC PALACE WITH ULTRAMODERN FURNISHINGS

PERA PALACE HOTEL

This luxuriously appointed hotel is based in a wonderful historic palace and despite being equipped with all the latest technology and gadgets it still exudes a nostalgic charme. The rooms all feature candelabra made from Murano glass, wooden floors and marble bathtubs; they boast elegant furnishings and exclusive fabrics. The hotel's restaurant serves delicious dishes from the best of the Turkish, French and Italian cuisines.

Mesrutiyet Caddesi 52,
Tel +90 (0) 212 377 40 00,
www.perapalace.com

OLD TOWN AND EYÜP

Four Seasons Istanbul at Sultanahmet The 65 rooms and suites of this venerable neoclassical building are all grouped around a garden. In the spa area a whole range of massages and treatments is on offer. The restaurant has a cocktail bar and a café and is housed in a glass pavilion within the garden. Many of the tourist sights in the Old Town are only a few minutes walk away from the hotel.

Tevkifhane Sokak 1,
Tel +90 (0) 212 402 30 00,
www.fourseasons.com/istanbul

BEYOGLU/BEŞIKTAŞ/SARIYER

Çira an Palace Kempinski This hotel resembles an Ottoman palace. You can see the Bosphorus through the floor-length windows and from the balconies of the spacious rooms. Guests may expect a first-class service and an ambience of peace away from the bustle of the metropolis. As well as outdoor and indoor pool the hotel has its own spa area with whirlpool, Turkish hamam as well as rooms for massage and beauty treatments. The four first-class restaurants invite you on a culinary journey around the world.

Çira an Caddesi 32,
Tel +90 (0) 212 326 46 46,
www.kempinski.com/de/istanbul

Tomtom Suites Parquet flooring and high ceilings make the comfortable suites here feel very special. The bathrooms are modern interpretations of historic Turkish baths, and all equipped with Carrara marble. Enjoy the sunset on the terrace with some of the delicious tapas from the restaurant.

Bo azkesen Caddesi, Tomtom Kaptan Sokak 32,
Tel +90 (0) 212 292 49 49,
www.tomtomsuites.com

W Istanbul A historical but also beautifully renovated building, this elegant hotel is famed for its imaginative lighting, which impresses as soon as you enter the lobby. Some of the rooms even have a private garden. The luxury restaurant, Frederic's, spoils its gourmet guests with select ingredients such as caviar, oysters and truffles, while the Minyon Restaurant serves international food.

Suleyman Seba Caddesi 22,
Tel +90 (0) 212 381 21 21,
www.wistanbul.com.tr

Hotel Les Ottomans Istanbul This Turkish Feng Shui Hotel with a French name is housed in a restored palace. This is where style encounters luxury: handwoven carpets,

This former palace houses the Pera Palace Hotel.

four-poster beds, paintings, hamam and whirlpool create a superb well-feeling ambience. Its location on one of the prettiest spots on the Bosphorus is also just about perfect, and the views from the terrace have to be seen to be believed – as did many a famous hotel guest.
Muallim Naci Caddesi 68,
Tel +90 (0) 212 359 15 00,
www.lesottomans.com

The House Hotel Nişantaşi The 45 beautifully styled rooms of this designer hotel are spread over the five levels of the buildings. They are unfussy in their appointments but very comfortable. Hues of white and brown predominate in the furnishings. Breakfast is served on the terrace, and the top floor is home to the hotel's bar. The hotel's location in the middle of a shopping and entertainment district is another bonus not to be forgotten.

Abdi Ipekçi Caddesi 34,
Tel +90 (0) 212 224 59 99,
www.thehousehotel.com

Witt Istanbul Suites As a guest in one of the 60 sq m (646 sq ft) suites you won't feel like you are staying at a hotel, but rather in a trendy loft apartment. Retro features and floral motifs complement the minimalist-modern furnishings. Marble cooking niches boasting espresso machines, steam baths, floor-length windows and XXL-sized beds are all much-appreciated elements. There are great views too from the fourth floor.
Defterdar Yokusu 26,
Tel +90 (0) 212 293 15 00,
www.wittistanbul.com

Swissôtel The Bosphorus All 600 rooms and suites are luxuriously appointed and impress with their exclusivity. The furniture is based on European models. The restaurants as well as the fitness and spa area leave no wish unfulfilled. The hotel also offers its guest a limousine service.
Bayildim Caddesi 2,
Tel +90 (0) 216 326 11 00,
www.swisshotel.com

ASIAN SIDE

Divan Istanbul Asia This 25-floor hotel is one of the most sought-after places on the Asian side of Istanbul, and it's popular not only with business people. The guests' comfort is of the utmost importance here. The spa area offers everything that you might look for to relax and chill out after an exciting day in the bustling city. The nearly 800-sq-m (8,608-sq-ft) ballroom is occasionally used as a venue for events.
Karayolu üzeri 209,
Tel +90 (0) 216 625 00 00,
www.divan.com.tr

The Sidamara Sarcophagus, a Roman columnar sarcophagus, is thought to date from around AD 250 and is on display in the Archaeological Museum.

MAJOR MUSEUMS

It is not only the mosques and palaces of Istanbul that hold great appeal for admirers of Islamic art and culture, the museum collections are also world class in terms of their quality and highlights. This is true of both the Museum for Turkish and Islamic Art as well as the Cinili Kösk next to the Archaeological Museum. The latter boasts an impressive collection of important oriental antiquities, whereas the Pera Museum is a must for anyone interested in the Orient. They are all outclassed by the Top-kapı Palace, however, home of the sultans for 400 years, with its magnificent rooms and top-class museum collections.

MAJOR MUSEUMS

The expansive Topkapı Palace complex features not only magnificent ceremonial rooms, the sultan's private chambers, luxuriously decorated harem apartments, government buildings, the palace school and settings for historic events, it also comprises valuable museum collections of Chinese and European porcelain, glass and silverware, sultans' robes, portraits of sultans and princes, the highly venerated Muslim reliquaries from the Prophet Mohammed and the treasury. These fascinating collections are distributed throughout the palace complex, with the former court kitchens and bakery in the second courtyard, for instance, having been converted into exhibition rooms. The costume collection and the treasury, like the reliquary chamber, form part of the third courtyard. You can visit the palace on a guided tour and then wander through the grounds and the courtyards.

COPPER AND BRASS TABLEWARE

Most of the objects on display were used at court for serving meals to at least 5,000 people daily. This number could be considerable greater on festive occasions. Most of the platters, bowls, pitchers, rose water dispensers, and other dishes are made of copper or tombac, a brass alloy with a copper content of more than 70 per cent, which is also referred to as gold brass. The exhibits (dating from the 16th to 19th centuries) are on display in the former court bakery.

EUROPEAN GLASS AND PORCELAIN

The valuable tableware also features various items of European manufacture, most of them diplomatic gifts that had been presented to the Ottoman court. These also include characteristic porcelain figures in oriental dress. Most of the collection's glassware, dating from the 17th to 19th centuries, originally came from Bohemia, but also from France, England and Russia.

ISTANBUL GLASS AND PORCELAIN

The collection on display in the former palace kitchens comprises some 2,000 or so items. Sultan Selim III (1789–1807) sent Mehmet Dede to Venice especially to learn the art of glassblowing in Murano. Dede's early work still reflected these techniques but he soon developed his own style. Porcelain was produced in Istanbul itself from about the mid-19th century, with the best-known manufacturer, in production from about 1890, being housed in the Yildiz Palace.

THE WEAPONS COLLECTION

The some 52,000 weapons making up the collection here cover a period of around 1,300 years and represent one of the most important weapons collections in the world. Most of the pieces were in the private possession of sultans and dignitaries, but many items in the collection were also gifts or the spoils of war. They originate from throughout the Islamic world and the collection also includes European and even Japanese weapons.

SULTANS' PORTRAITS

All thirty-six Ottoman sultans as of 1299 are represented in this collection but it is only from the time of Sultan Mehmed II (1451 to 1481) that they can really be referred to as portraits. The sultans from before the time of his reign

Left: A gate and gateway at the Topkapı Palace, elaborately decorated with arabesques.
Below: Constantinople, now Istanbul, was conquered in 1453 by Sultan Mehmed II.

CHINESE PORCELAIN

Ceramics with a transparent glaze were known in China from about the 2nd century BC and genuine porcelain was developed between about AD 500 and 1000. This was the Seladon porcelain with a green-blue glaze dating from the Sung dynasty (960 to 1279) and constituting the first period of classical Chinese porcelain. The restrained decoration featured plants and geometric patterns but the esthetic value lay primarily in the shape of the pieces. Shade differentiation and much more elaborate ornamentation then followed during the Yuan dynasty (1280–1368). During the Ming

were portrayed retrospectively on the basis of oral descriptions or else as purely from imagination. The techniques used extend from engravings to watercolors through to oil paintings. The majority of them are the work of Ottoman miniaturists but there are also works by European artists.

THE SULTANS' ROBES

One of the buildings that used to be part of the baths houses a splendid collection of sultans' robes, shoes, headwear such as turbans and also the fez head cover in use as of 1827. These velvet and silk fabrics were at one time the attire of sultans, princes and princesses. The oldest pieces on display here date from the 15th century. A great many of the robes are easily dated because they also appear in the portraits of the rulers.

CHINESE AND JAPANESE PORCELAIN

One of the Topkapı Palace's most valuable treasures is a collection of more than 10,000 items of Chinese and Japanese porcelain, including the collection of the Shah of Persia looted in the 16th century. Indeed, the Topkapı Palace houses the largest collection of Chinese porcelain outside of China. There is no better place to follow the development of Chinese porcelain from the 13th to 20th centuries.

THE RELIQUARY CHAMBER

Memorabilia from the Prophet Mohammed were also housed in the sultans' private apartments, most of them finding their way to the sultan's court as gifts. The reliquaries from Medina were also brought to Istanbul during World War I. The most valuable items include the Prophet's holy cloak, kept in a golden shrine, as well as flags, bows and Mohammed's sword. Also kept in the Reliquary Chamber is hair from the Prophet's beard, one of his teeth, his seal, letters and his footprint. The chamber also houses the swords of the first four caliphs, the Koran of the Caliph Osman and a door from the Great Mosque in Mecca. The Staff of Moses, King David's sword and the Rock of Joseph date back to the Old Testament. There are also items of memorabilia relating to Fatima, Mohammed's daughter.

THE TREASURY

The treasury is housed in the very heart of the palace complex. Many of the items came to the sultans' court as gifts but a great number were also

TOPKAPI SERAIL MUSEUMS

dynasty (1368–1644), the first golden age occurred with a preference for blue-white decoration, splendid colors and a high degree of luster. Chinese porcelain enjoyed the last of its golden ages under the Manchu emperors (1644 to 1912).

Chinese porcelain

the spoils of the various wars. The diverse range of objects extends from mail shirts decorated with precious stones and decorative weapons through to sultan's thrones and precious stone jewelry, from lamps and vessels to writing utensils. The highlights include the "Spoonmaker's Diamond" (86 carats), as well as the head and arm reliquary of John the Baptist, who is venerated by Muslims as well.

Topkapı Sarayi, Sarayii,
Sultanahmet
Tel +90 (0) 212 512 0480
www.kultur.gov.tr
Wed–Mon 9.00–17.00.

A gem-encrusted teapot

MAJOR MUSEUMS

The museum complex in Gülhane Park beneath the Topkapı Palace comprises not only the Archaeological Museum but also the former art academy building housing the Museum of the Ancient Orient and the ceramic museum in the Cinili Kösk. The Cinili Kösk, a garden pavilion built in 1472 with filigree arcades on the atrium façade, dating from the 18th century, and the splendid glazed wall tiles on the inside, is considered the oldest surviving secular Ottoman building in Istanbul. In the 19th century the Cinili Kösk, or Tiled Kiosk, housed the archaeological collection before this was housed in a separate building in 1896, namely the present neoclassical building designed by the architect Alexander Vallaury (the Old Museum). The appearance of the museum's façade is inspired by the sarcophagi on display inside. A modern extension (the New Museum) was added in the 1970s.

THE HISTORY OF THE COLLECTION

The antiquities collection belonging to the Minister of War, Fethi Ahmet Pasha, son-in-law of Sultan Mahmut II, on display in the Hagia Eirene, a former Byzantine church, since 1846, forms the basis of the museum's inventory. The collection was converted into a court museum and grew rapidly with the addition of artifacts from throughout the territories of the former Ottoman Empire. It was already prohibited at that time to remove archaeological finds from the country. The Antiquities collection was transferred to the Cinili Kösk in 1875 for space reasons. The industrious painter and archaeologist Osman Hamdi Bey took on responsibility for the collection in 1881 and, through his own excavation work in Sidon (present-day Lebanon), he procured some of the collection's most valuable objects, including the Alexander Sarcophagus and the Sarcophagus of the Crying Women. The collection was also converted to a museum open to the public under Hamdi Bey and he was able to undertake the long overdue construction of a new building for the museum.

THE OLD MUSEUM

The great many Greek, Roman and Oriental sarcophagi on display in the neoclassical main building are certainly the museum's main attraction. In addition to the prized and world-famous Alexander Sarcophagus, one of the other especially remarkable exhibits is the Sarcophagus of the Crying Women dating from around 350 BC in the form of an Ionian temple with 18 women between its columns lamenting the dead, its roof decorated with funeral processions,. Both objects were excavated by Osman Hamdi Bey in 1887 in the necropolis of Sidon in Phoenicia (today Sidon in the Lebanon) together with other valuable artifacts. The Pergamon bust of Alexander is also worth seeing. It is a copy dating from the first half of the 2nd century BC of the original by the sculptor Lysipp (4th cenury BC). The classical Greek grave stelae (5th century BC), the numerous busts, including very many of the Roman emperors, as well as statues and architectural fragments going back to the Byzantine era make up some of the museum's main treasures.

THE NEW MUSEUM

The lower floor of the new building is dedicated to exhibits from Byzantium and

THE ARCHAEOLOGICAL MUSEUM

Left and below: Part of the Archaeological Museum is reserved for the many Roman statues, busts and sculptures.

MAJOR MUSEUMS

THE ALEXANDER SARCOPHAGUS

The museum's most famous exhibit is the Alexander Sarcophagus that owes its name to the battle portrayed on one of the long sides between the Greeks under the leadership of the heroic Macedonian king, Alexander the Great, and their opponents, the Persians. The other long side depicts a lion hunt, while the short sides feature a further battle scene and a panther hunt. Dating from around 320/310 BC, the Alexander Sarcophagus is a splendid example of early Hellenic sculpture and is in fact considered the best surviving example of an ancient sarcophagus. The overall construction of the

Thrace, include relief carvings, ivory, gold work and mosaics. The ground floor focuses on the history of the city of Istanbul. The objects cover a time period extending from the early Stone Age through to the Byzantine era, with busts, sarcophagi, a group of statues from a Roman fountain, coins, gold jewelry and Christian mosaics on display. The upper floor exhibits largely comprise artifacts from the Anatolian region, including an Anatolian burial chamber and numerous items such as urns and gold jewelry, but also building models from ancient Troy. The top floor, however, is dedicated to present-day excavation finds from the adjoining regions of Syria, Lebanon, Palestine and Cyprus that once formed part of the Ottoman Empire. The Archaeological Museum also features a dedicated section for children in this building.

THE MUSEUM OF THE ANCIENT ORIENT

The most important exhibits in this museum are dedicated to pre-Islamic art and in fact form a department of the Archaeological Museum. The collection here comprises artifacts originating from ancient Mesopotamia (comprising parts of present-day Iraq, Iran, Syria and Turkey), particularly from the Babylonian and Assyrian eras, Hittite, Egyptian and Arab Antiquities, as well as objects from the Mari civilization. Idols, statues, bas-reliefs, seals, glazed bricks, tools and inscriptions are surviving testimony to these early civilizations. They include painted papyrus rolls, mummy masks and a reclining sphinx from Egypt, statues of gods from Mari (modern Tell Hariri in Syria), marble carvings from Assyrian royal palaces, as well as a carved

dragon and lions from the Processional Way and the Ishtar Gate in Babylon commissioned by Nebuchadnezzar II (6th century BC). You can also trace the development of the cuneiform script from the 3rd to the 1st millenniums BC here. A particular highlight is the fragment in Hittite cuneiform script from the peace treaty concluded in 1259 BC between the Hittite King Hattusili II and the Egyptian Pharaoh Ramesses II following the Battle of Kadesh.

THE CINILI KÖSK MUSEUM

With its equally valuable architecture the rooms of this museum house a remarkable collection of Ottoman ceramics. Tiles, lamps for use in mosques, bowls and platters in splendid hues and with patterns comprising flowers, vines, geometric motifs and some even with

THE ARCHAEOLOGICAL MUSEUM

sarcophagus resembles the shape of a Greek temple. The almost three-dimensional carved figures on the sarcophagus' sides are very lifelike and exude a vitality that was accentuated by the shades and hues of the original version.

The Alexander Sarcophagus

landscapes or calligraphic letters are on display. There is even a *mihrab*, a prayer niche facing toward Mecca and a customary feature in mosques, on display, one that comes from the Ibrahim Bey Mosque in Karaman. The oldest exhibits date from the Seljuk era (12th to 14th centuries). Those works from the Ottoman period are from the 16th to 19th centuries and include a great many vessels and tiles from Iznik.

Arkeoloji Müzesi,
Osman Hamdi Bey Yokusu
Sokak Gülhane,
Tel +90 (0) 212 520 77 40,
Tue–Sun 9.00–17.00.

Antiquities from ancient Egypt

The former palace of the Grand Vizier Halil Ibrahim Pasha located close to the Hippodrome and the Blue Mosque today houses an interesting collection of Turkish and Islamic art. The palace was assigned to the Grand Vizier in 1524 on the occasion of his marriage to the sister of Sultan Süleyman the Magnificent. The splendor of this unusual stone building soon overshadowed all other palaces in the city. The sultan had the very powerful Grand Vizier murdered in 1536, however, probably for reasons relating to a plot by the sultan's wife, Roxelana, who allegedly denounced him as a traitor. All of the Grand Vizier's possessions were confiscated and his palace subsequently served as government offices for a range of dignitaries. The palace was later appropriated for use as a prison and also as a textile factory, among other purposes, and the building eventually fell into disrepair as a result.

THE HISTORY OF THE COLLECTION

When, from the 19th century, attention was paid to the collecting of antiquities in the Ottoman Empire, too, the focus was not solely on Antiquity and ancient civilizations, but also on the treasures of Islam's own cultural past. Most of these treasures were owned by mosques, madrasahs and religious foundations and, consequently, the then minister Hayri Efendi initiated efforts as of 1909 to have an appropriate museum established, this subsequently being opened to the public in 1914.

The museum was initially based in the former kitchens of the Süleymaniye Mosque. In 1983, parts of the Ibrahim Pasha Palace were made available to the museum and today it is one of the world's leading museums of its kind. The exhibits on show here date back in age to the 7th century.

THE COLLECTIONS

Dedicated to the applied arts and to craftwork, the museum is arranged according to the materials used, the topographic areas of production and the various style periods. In particular, it provides insight into the way of life of the nomadic and Turkic peoples, as well as displaying age-old handicraft techniques. Also on display are the characteristic interiors of Islamic tradition and the nomad felt tents (yurts).

CARPETS

The museum possesses the oldest surviving carpets in the world as well as the largest collection of historic carpets worldwide. These include rare Seljuk knotted carpets and kelims (woven carpets), particularly the Konya carpets dating from the 12th century and thus predating the Ottoman Empire. Forming part of the Turkic tribes, the Seljuks brought the art of carpet-making to Asia Minor. The museum also has Anatolian carpets (15th to 17th centuries), including Usak carpets and those known in Europe as "Holbein carpets", their pattern comprising a basic geometric structure. Persian and Caucasian carpets – the latter being largely Armenian from Karabakh – are further features of the collection that also includes prayer mats.

MINIATURES AND MANUSCRIPTS

In addition to deeds and decrees with complex calligraphic signatures by the sultans and Persian miniature paintings, the museum's most remarkable

THE MUSEUM OF TURKISH AND ISLAMIC ART

Left: The exterior of the museum building, a former palace from the 16th century
Below: Ornate woven carpets from the Ottoman era.

ISLAMIC CERAMICS

Islam prohibits the depiction of either God or other individuals in the religious context. An elaborate ornamental art thus developed as a substitute for the pictorial recounting of religious narratives, deriving its wealth of motifs from both nature and geometry. Mosques, palaces and the like were decorated with a wall cladding of glazed ceramics that soon came to exhibit an overwhelming wealth of bright patterns. Luster painting was already known during the Abbasid period (750–1258), with ceramics being given a shimmering, metallic luster as a result of a fired coating comprising a

treasures include Qu'ranic manuscripts from throughout the Qu'ran's area of circulation and dating from its origins in the 7th century through to the 20th century. One of the special treasures is a parchment manuscript in Kufic script, later the obligatory script for the Qu'ran, from the second half of the 7th century.

CERAMICS AND GLASS

On display in the museum are wall tiles from the Seljuk period onward, their early geometric patterns having been comprised of tiny pieces of tiles just like a mosaic. Of particular importance, however, was the production of glazed pottery in the Ottoman period that followed, one of the main centers of production being the town of Iznik in western Anatolia. The bright hues and wealth of

flowers are indeed an eye-catching feature. In the Ottoman Empire the preference was mostly for the production of larger, square tiles with a white background decorated with elaborately colored vines and later with flower decorations. Iznik, in the present-day province of Bursa, became the ceramic center where blue decoration, vines, arabesques and Kufic inscriptions were especially characteristic of the first period, from about 1490 to 1525, then followed by flower motifs until about 1555, particularly featuring carnations and bluebells. In the last period, from around the middle of the 16th through to the 18th centuries, the tile patterns were further characterized by the depiction of tulips, roses, hyacinths and other plants, as well as by generally bright colors. The museum thus provides a comprehensive insight into

the production of ceramic mosaics, lamps and vessels. There are also tiles depicting the holy sites in Mecca on display. The museum also has early Islamic glass from the 9th century.

TEXTILES AND EMBROIDERY

The particular highlights in these departments are the sultan's shirts which are decorated with Qu'ran inscriptions.

WOOD

The 9th-century carvings from Anatolia also provide an insight into Islam's fondness for ornament. The exhibits here are often beautifully embellished with mother-of-pearl, ivory or tortoiseshell inlays, these including Qu'ran reading stands, Qu'ran bindings, Qu'ran holders, caskets, wooden doors and window shutters.

silver-copper alloy. This technique was further developed under the Seljuks and the Ottoman Empire with tiles and vessels being produced in vibrant colors and with elaborate flower motifs.

Ornamental ceramic art

STONE

In this department, it is tombstones, carvings and panels with inscriptions that attract the visitor's attention.

METAL

The museum's inventory also includes art and handicrafts made from silver, gold, brass and other metals. Door knockers, weights, copper tableware, pestle and mortars, mirrors, rosewater flacons and candlesticks from the Seljuk period provide an insight into the luxurious way of life at the courts of the Orient.

Türk ve Islam Eserleri Müzesi, Ibrahim Pasa, At Meydani 46, Tel +90 (0) 212 518 18 05, Tue–Sun 9.30–17.30.

Gilded copper coffeepot (1870).

Situated in the Tepebaşi district, known as Pera to the Ancient Greeks, this private museum is housed in what was formerly the Hotel Bristol. This magnificent historical building was built in 1893 and designed by the Greek architect Achille Manousos. Only the splendid original façade still survives as the interior of the building has been completely demolished. This enabled the creation of five floors for the new, modern museum building which opened to the public in 2005. The two lower floors house the permanent exhibition as well as accommodating items from the Sevgi Gönül and Erdogan Gallery. Temporary exhibitions by prominent classical and modern artists are staged on the upper three floors, dedicated multi-purpose exhibition spaces, where films are also shown and a great many other cultural activities are on offer. The basement has a lobby and an auditorium for lectures.

THE HISTORY OF THE COLLECTION

The Pera Museum is run by the Suna & Inan Kiraç Foundation. Suna Kiraç is a member of the Koç family, one of the wealthiest families in the whole of Turkey. She is the daughter of Vehbi Koç, the company's founder. The business empire was established in the 1920s and is now known as the Koç Holding, an international corporation comprising nearly one hundred separate companies, active in a number of different sectors and the largest conglomerate in Turkey. The family has always been committed to the sponsorship of culture and especially to education in general, as well as to health issues. In Istanbul a further family foundation also sponsors the Rahmi M Koç Museum, the largest museum of technology in Turkey. The Sadberg Hanim Museum in Istanbul displays some of the treasures from the Koç family's private art collection. The overall Suna & Inan Kiraç Foundation complex also includes a cultural and a research center. A new building designed by the American star architect Frank O Gehry is being built for the Suna Kiraç Cultural Center close to the museum. The permanent exhibits in the Pera Museum include a ceramics collection, a collection of Anatolian weights, the Erdogan Gallery with its temporary exhibitions and an oriental painting collection.

KÜTAHYA TILES AND CERAMICS

The city of Kütahya, the capital of the province of the same name between Bursa and Ankara, was one of the most important ceramic centers in the Ottoman Empire during the 16th and 17th centuries. The city has been able to retain its handicraft tradition through the ages and traditional tiles and porcelain are still produced there today. The Pera Museum's exhibits comprising fancifully styled tiles and vessels provide an overview of this production and its history and are also an attempt to further promote this manufacturing center which has always been overshadowed by Iznik.

ANATOLIAN WEIGHTS

This section displays weights and measuring instruments from the Anatolian Highlands. Made using a wide variety of techniques, materials and shapes, these fascinating instruments date back to the beginnings of early history and provide an unusual insight into the history of measuring and weighing in Anatolia.

THE PERA MUSEUM

Left: The collection of paintings transfixes most observers.
Below: The facade of the late 19th-century museum building.

ORIENTALISM

No longer feeling themselves to be under threat from the Turks, in the 18th century the Europeans discovered the aesthetic appeal of the Middle East. An overwhelming fascination with the Orient followed Napoleon's Egyptian campaign of 1798. The tales of *One Thousand and One Nights*, often known as the *Arabian Nights*, were first translated between 1704 and 1714, and artists, poets and intellectuals began journeying to the Orient even prior to 1850. World exhibitions introduced Oriental art and architecture to Europe and by 1900 Orientalism had become tremendously fashion-

ORIENTAL PAINTING COLLECTION

The museum's unique collection of paintings from the 17th to the 19th centuries provides detailed insights into the world of the Orient in the past, particularly as seen from a European perspective. The oldest paintings attempt to document this – to Westerners – alien world, while the later paintings also freely indulge in European romantic notions of a sensual and intoxicating Orient. Some artists journeyed with delegations as chroniclers, so to speak, whereas others became court painters and yet others still simply undertook a journey to the Orient off their own back. The collection's most important works include the *Woman in Turkish Dress* by Jean-Etienne Liotard (1702–1789), a Swiss-French rococo artist working in pastels, who

spent the years 1738 to 1743 in Constantinople. He "went native" and lived there as a Turk himself and, when he returned, he brought back with him many paintings and drawings recording his impressions of the Ottoman Empire.

Other works depict portraits of sultans, princes, dignitaries and envoys or audiences with foreign ambassadors in the sultan's palace, oriental women and harem scenes, as well as views of the city and scenes from life in the Ottoman Empire. They include those by Jean-Baptiste van Mour and Antoine de Favray, two 18th-century French painters, by Fausto Zonaro, an Italian painter from the Padua area and who was the sultan's court artist in around 1900, and by Jules Joseph Lefebvre, a French salon artist and art teacher at the end of the 19th century. Recently acquired for a very

high price at an auction, the museum is today especially proud of *The Tortoise Trainer* (1906) by Osman Hamdy Bey, an outstanding representative of European Orientalism, with another five works by the same master being on display in the Pera Museum.

The painter was born in Constantinople in 1842 as the son of the Ottoman envoy to the imperial court in Vienna and later Grand Vizier Edhem Pasha. Like his father, Hamdy Bey also began a diplomatic career initially, but in about 1870 he decided to abandon this career path to study painting in Paris instead. He was also active as an archaeologist and in 1887 excavated Sidon, part of the Ottoman Empire at the time. In 1881 Hamdy Bey was appointed director of what was later to become the Archaeological Museums. The artist did a great deal to pre-

THE PERA MUSEUM

able. Clothing, interior décor and glittering images of life in the Orient were highly sought-after. Even modernist painters and architects drew inspiration from the hues and the white, cubic buildings of the Orient.

Genre painting from the Ottoman period

serve and promote the cultural heritage of the Ottoman Empire and for establishing and maintaining artistic contacts with the West. Hamdy Bey's works in the style of European Orientalism provide detailed accounts of everyday life in the Ottoman Empire. He never succumbed to the florid imaginings of some Europeans and so his paintings also became a valuable and credible documentation of cultural history.

Pera Museum, Mesrutiyet Caddesi No. 66, Tel +90 (0) 212 334 99 00, www.peramuzesi.org.tr, Tue–Sat 10.00–19.00, Sun 12.00–18.00.

The Tortoise Trainer, by Osman Hamdy Bey (1906)

The two-level Galata Bridge spanning the Golden Horn was completed in 1992.

Despite its immense size, the city is easy to explore on foot. Walking the city will allow you to experience different aspects of this historic town. Many of the most interesting buildings can be found in the Old Town – here stand the most exciting mosques and palaces, fountains and bazaars making fairy tales from 1001 nights come vividly to life. Let yourself drift through the mix of magnificent boulevards and narrow alleyways which is so typical of the Orient. Make sure you also enjoy the vibrant bustle of the markets on the other side of the Golden Horn, where tea and coffeehouses invite you to linger at almost every corner.

Ancient masterpieces of sculpture can be admired at the Archaeological Museum.

SIGHTS

 Topkapı Palace The palace, built in the 15th century as the seat of government was initially the political heart of the Ottoman world. Today the complex houses several first-rate collections (incuding silver and glassware, ceramics, jewelry and robes), all of which impressibly document the glory of that period. Despite its exceptional significance, the Topkapı Palce is almost graceful in its architecture. The courtyards in between the various buildings are perfectly suited for leisurely strolling.

Archaeological Museum One of the most important exhibition pieces at this renowned museum is the world-famous Alexande Sarcophagus, whose reliefs depict Alexander the Great in a battle against the Persians. Also on show are further works of art from Antiquity, including items made from clay and glazed tiles as well as objects from the history of Istanbul.

Hagia Eirene The Byzantine church, dating from the sixth century, was built on the foundations of an earlier structure. After the conquest of Constantinople by the Ottomans in 1453, the church was used as a weapons arsenal for a while and in the subsequent period it served several times as a museum. Thanks to its outstanding acoustics the Hagia Eirene has regularly been a venue for concerts in recent decades.

Sultan Ahmet Fountain For many locals as well as for visitors to Istanbul this is the most beautiful fountain in the city. An outstanding example of Turkish fountain architecture, The Sultan Ahmet Fountain is adorned with beautiful floral reliefs and features decorated marble basins, artistically forged fencing and five small domes. Also worth seeing are the calligraphic inscriptions above the water spouts.

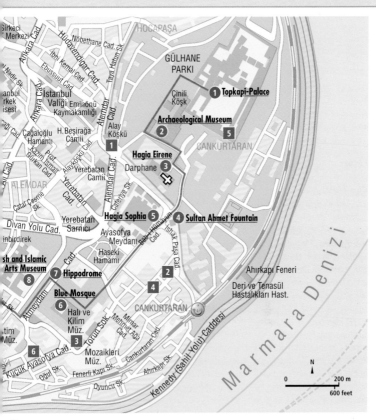

5 Hagia Sophia The historic building looking back on more than 1,400 years of history is one of the most striking landmarks in Istanbul, dominating the cityscape with its slender minarets. The magnificent document of the Byzantine art of building was converted into a mosque in the 15th century by the Ottomans. Hardly a visitor will be able to resist the fascinating apperance of the main nave ending in a 56-m-high (184-ft) dome. Inside, the Hagia Sophia is also home to art-historically important mosaics, which adorn entire sections of walls and ceiling.

6 Blue Mosque This famous sacred building owes its name to the predominant color of the interior furnishings. Also

The blue tiles that adorn the dome and some of the walls in the Sultan Ahmed Mosque are what gave it the name by which it is known in Europe.

known as the Sultan Ahmed Mosque, this structure is remarkable in more ways than one – few other mosques can boast six minarets, the forecourt is virtually unique in its vast extent, and the decoration of the interior rooms with (blue) tiles is unparalleled. Many of the more than 200 windows in the mosque are also glazed in blue. The outside is spellbinding to see especially when illuminated at night.

❼ Hippodrome There is little left in the hippodrome, dating from the third century, to remind us today of its original purpose as a stadium. Up to 100,000 spectators are said to have watched the contests here in Antiquity, such as the daredevil chariot races that once took place here. Only few architectural remains are preserved of this former complex, including some of the columns,

which had been brought here from foreign countries: the Egyptian obelisk, boasting remarkable reliefs, hails from Luxor, the snake column from Delphi. The cobbled road approximately follows the course of the earlier race track.

❽ Turkish and Islamic Arts Museum With the help of around 40,000 exhibits – starting in date from the early Islamic period and continuing up to the present day – visitors are presented with a cross-section of the artistic and artisanal production in the regions of Asia Minor. Among the highlights at the museum is its amazing collection of carpets, which includes many magnificent and valuable pieces to be admired. The tents of nomads in Anatolia are also worth seeng; they document a lifestyle that is still very much alive there today.

❾ Sokullu Mehmed Paşa Mosque Built in 1572 for the Grand Vizier Sokullu Mehmed Paşa, this mosque was erected on a slope above a madrasah. From the outside it is hard to imahine the splendor that will greet you inside. Faïences extending right up to the ceiling cover some of the walls. Together with the stained-glass windows they provide the inner rooms with an impressive display of colorful lights.

SHOPPING

▮ Cafer Aga Courtyard Away from the hectic bustle of the main shopping streets you can stroll between the stalls in this tranquil courtyard in peace and quiet. Built in 1559 and initially used as a madrasah, it now has a selection of crafts items, jewelry, ceramics and calligraphies for sale directly from the producer.

THE MOST MAGNIFICENT BUILDINGS

The view from the terrace of the Seven Hills Restaurant is just as wonderful as its fish dishes.

Caferiye Sokak,
Tel +90 (0) 212 513 18 43,
8.30–20.00 daily.

2 **Istanbul Handicrafts Center** Here you can watch how clay pots, pipes, jewelry, dolls and calligraphies are made and how books are bound. There is probably no other place in Istanbul where Turkish handicrafts are presented in as impressive a manner as they are here. All the newly created products are of course for sale as well.
Kabasakal Caddesi 5,
Tel +90 (0) 212 517 67 82,
9.30–17.30 daily.

3 **Arasta Çarşisi** This street, which is home to a museum of mosaics, is lined by several shops and stalls where handicrafts items are sold at first hand. This is probably also a good place for you to find a souvenir of your visit. The rich selection of carpets is also worth seeing. The quality of the items for sale in this street is also generally noticeably higher that that available at some of the Istanbul bazaars.
9.00–20.00 daily.

EATING AND DRINKING

4 **Seven Hills Restaurant** Located on the top floor of the Seven Hills Hotel, this place boasts to be the best fish restaurant in town. All the dishes are prepared from what has been freshly caught that day in the Sea of Marmara. Its opulent fresh seafood platters are always a particular hit with diners. Make sure you ask for a place on the terrace when you book – the view from here across the city and the sea is abolutely fabulous.
Tevkifhane Sokak 27,
Tel +90 (0) 212 516 94 97,
www.hotelsevenhills.com

5 **Konyali** Located in the grounds of the Topkapı Palace, this restaurant is now being run by the same family in the fourth generation. Many well-known heads of state have been served her. The chefs who cook according to traditonal Turkish recipes are considered masters of their trade.
Topkapı Palace,
Tel +90(0) 212 513 96 96,
www.konyalilokantasi.com

6 **Türkistan Aşevi** Dating from the Ottoman period, this villa near the Sultan Ahmed Mosque is furnished with carpets and fabrics from that time. The menu lists numerous dishes from Central Asia. It often includes pancakes with a variety of different delicious fillings. Alcohol, however, is not for sale at this establishment.
Tavukhane Sokak 36,
Tel +90 (0) 212 638 65 25,
www.turkistanasevi

The upturned head of the Medusa in the Cistern of 1,001 Columns, which was once an important water storage place.

SIGHTS

❶ Binbirdirek Sarnici This complex, which is also known under the name of the "Cistern of 1,001 Columns", was built as early as the fourth century AD and was at that time one of the largest water storage reservoirs in the city. The number of columns is a grossly exaggerated of course, but nevertheless the structure is held up by 264 columns. A visit once used to be a difficult undertaking and was open only for the bravest of tourists, yet today the cistern is a very lively shopping mall comprising many different stalls and stores.

❷ Sultan Mahmut II's Tomb This octagonal mausoleum was built in 1838 – one year before the death of Sultan Mahmut II. Aside from his tomb it is also home to the burial resting places of several

other sultans. The mausoleum is remarkable for the rich pictorial decoration of the internal walls, which are supported by Corinthian columns. The mausoleum is situated within a small cemetery where you can find further tombs that are impressive testimonies of Turkish stone masonry art.

❸ Column of Constantine No other structure in Istanbul is older than this column, which was erected in 330 on the occasion of the promotion – by Emperor Constantine – of Byzantium as the new capital of the Roman Empire. Before that date, the column made from porphyry was crowned by a statue of Emperor Constantine; however, this was destroyed by a hurricane in the year 1106. The shaft of the column was still standing and it was preserved and strengthened by metal rings. UNfortu-

nately it was damaged on several occasions by large fires, and this can today still be seen from its dark coloration.

❹ Atik Ali Paşa Mosque Built in 1496, this mosque was named after the Grand Vizier

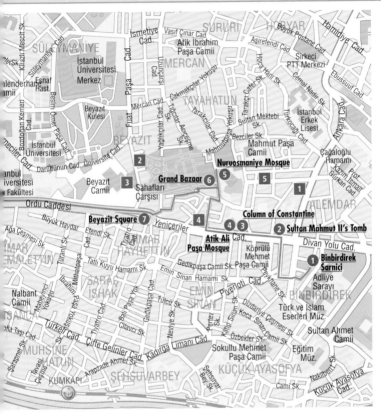

Atik Ali Paşa and it is certainly one of the oldest religious Islamic edifices in the city. The mosque is surrounded by walls and its 24-m-high (79-ft) dome is flanked by two smaller side-domes. The cemetery located outside the mosque is the final resting place for several Muslim spiritual leaders.

⑤ Nuruosmaniye Mosque
The mosque was finished in 1755 after a construction period of seven years. The mosque has dome with a diameter of 26 m (85 ft), and underneath it several rows of windows that allow the light to illuminate the interior. The mighty arches supporting the dome are remarkable. Inside, there is an impressive wooden frieze carved with calligraphies. The Nuruos-

The vast Grand Bazaar comprises numerous shops and stalls selling myriad different goods.

maniye Mosque (literally: "The Light of Osman") also has a Qur'anic school and a library.

6 **Grand Bazaar** Gates from all the directions of the compass lead into this absolutely gigantic bazaar, which should without doubt feature on the must-see program of every visit to Istanbul. There are numerous signs designed to make it easier for people to orientate but many a visitor has already lost his way in this maze of lanes and alleyways. Here you can see and experience the entire range of Oriental handicrafts – fabrics and textiles, gold and silver jewelry, leatherware, carpets and much, much more will all exchange ownership here. In addition there are antiques, housewares and souvenirs for sale. Several coffeehouses and tearooms provide refreshments and a break from the often hectic surroundings.

7 **Beyazit Square** It is not only the fleamarket taking place here every day that attracts the tourists. On the eastern side of the square stands the Beyazit Mosque completed in 1506. Its inner courtyard, surrounded by arcades, boasts several fountains and is paved in polychrome marble. For the furnishings of the interior, the Hagia Sophia served as a model. On its northern side, the Beyazit Square is bounded by the monumental entrance to the University of Istanbul.

8 **Bodrum Mosque** This mosque was converted from a Byzantine church dating from the 10th century. The brick-built façade and the many windows and openings allowing light to enter the dome still attest to its earlier function. The edifice was used as a mosque from as early as the 15th century. The original furnishings were largely destroyed by serious fires. The name refers to its substructure (*bodum* in Turkish).

9 **Tulip Mosque** Completed in 1769, this mosque is considered an outstanding example of the Turkish baroque style. The ambience of the interior spaces is dominated by marble in almost all hues (including yellow, red and a bluish gray). Remarkable is the hall in the mosque's cellar which serves as a market hall where mostly clothing is sold. The name of the mosque is derived from the era at the beginning of the 18th century known as the "Tulip Period", when the sultans expressed a love for tulips in their horticultural designs resulting in a worldwide craze.

SHOPPING

1 **Sofa** Calligraphies are one of the most expressive mani-

The Kurukahveci Mehmet Efendi Coffee Shop is highly rated with its clients for excellent coffee.

Katip Çelebi Caddesi 104,
Tel +90 (0) 212 519 49 22,
9.00–24.00 daily.

2 Tahtakale Caddesi A pure and unadulterated Arab market as one would imagine it takes place in this street. Other than in the Grand Bazaar, however, this market is entirely in the open air. The range of goods that are traded is enormous, from electrical appliances via small pieces of furniture to (cheap) clothing. Lively haggling for every item is par for the course here.

3 Spice Bazaar The atmosphere could hardly be more Oriental in feel: as the name suggests, spices are the main goods traded here. In addition you can also find dried fruit, all kinds of nuts, medicinal herbs and much more. Also known as the "Egyptian Bazaar", this market is one of the most pop-ular tourist attractions in Istanbul and a definite "must-see".
Cami Meydani Sokak,
Mon–Sat 8.00–19.00.

EATING AND DRINKING

4 Bulvar Palas This restaurant, based in the hotel of the same name, is open around the clock. Here guests are spoiled with specialties from Turkey and the regions and countries of the Mediterranean.
Atatürk Bulvar 36,
Tel +90 (0) 212 528 58 81,
www.hotelbulvarpalas.com,
24 hours a day

5 Darüzziyafe The former soup kitchen for the poor of the Sultan Süleyman Mosque is today home to a restaurant offering the culinary delights from the Ottoman era – including vegetable and meat soups. No alcohol is served at this restaurant, however.

Şifahane Caddesi 6,
Tel +90 (0) 212 511 84 14,
www.daruzziyafe.com.tr

6 Pandeli Founded in 1956 by a Greek man, the Pandeli is the oldest eatery in the Spice Bazaar. Particularly popular with its customers are grilled fish and poultry as well as egg-plant/aubergines in puff pastry.
Misir Çarflisi 1,
Tel +90 (0) 212 527 39 09,
www.pandeli.com.tr

7 Kurukahveci Mehmet Efendi One of Istanbul coffee-houses with a long tradition, the Turkish coffee that is served here is much appreciated by the locals. There is also a large se-lection of delicious desserts to have with it, and clients may take packets of the coffee home with them.
Tahmis Sokak 66,
Tel +90 (0) 212 511 42 62,
www.mehmetefendi.com

Fishing on the Galata Bridge. The Galata Tower can be made out in the background.

SIGHTS

1 Galata Bridge There are some cafés and restaurants situated on the lower, roofed deck, while the upper deck is open to the skies. The present Galata Bridge was built in 1992, on the site of an earlier bridge damaged by fire. It rests on a total of 114 piers, measures about 42 m (138 ft) wide and has been equipped with eight lanes to take the never-ending car traffic.

2 Yeralti Mosque This subterranean mosque is unique in Istanbul. It was built in 1757 on the site of an earlier castle which had however been demolished long before the construction of the mosque began. The mosque was sited in the former castle cellar that had once served as a weapons and munitions depot. It houses the tombs of two Muslim holy men, superbly decorated with faïences. Remarkable in architectural terms are its low vaults, supported by many gorgeous columns.

3 Arabic Mosque During the course of the Christian Reconquista in Spain, completed in 1492, many Muslim Moors (Arabs) fled from Spain to Istanbul. They were assigned a church that had probably been completed in 1260, and they redesigned it as a mosque which was named after them, Arabic Mosque. Even after adding a minaret and further alterations much remains that recalls the earlier Christian structure.

4 Galata Tower The Genoese, who had founded a colony here, built this tower in 1348 as a part of their fortifications. During the Ottoman era, too, it served as a watchtower. The round building has a conical roof and measures 62 m (203 ft) high. From the viewing platform, reached by elevator and a few steps, just below the top of the tower you can enjoy an overwhelming panoramic view of the city right up to the Princes' Islands.

5 Istiklal Caddesi The pedestrianized zone, served by a nostalgic tramway, extends up to Taksim and is one of the commercial centers in Beyoglu. This is where Istanbul can be seen from its most European side. The avenue is flanked by countless stores, restaurants and cafés as well as a few well-preserved historic buildings. Some of these grand edifices now serve as residences for consulates. The boulevard is well known for its nightlife: at weekends the Istiklal Caddesi gets so crowded it is hard to move along it at all.

THE HIGHLIGHTS OF BEYOĞLU

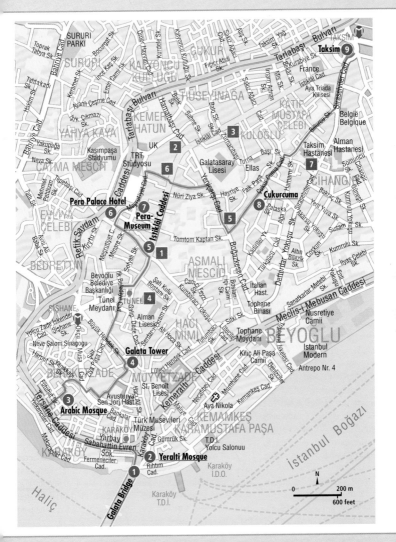

The Pera Palace Hotel Restaurant exudes the nostalgic charme of the late 19th century.

6 Pera Palace Hotel Even after several renovations the Pera Palace hotel still exudes the air of a truly "grand" hotel. Many famous people from politics as well as showbiz celebrities have stayed here to be pampered in the hotel that was originally opened in 1892 specifically to accommodate travelers on the Orient Express. Alongside the magnificent furnishings, the outside appearance of the palace is fascinating in its own way.

7 Pera Museum The modern cultural center, established in the former Bristol Hotel in 2005, exhibits art collections dating from the time of the Ottoman rulers right up to modernity. Worth seeing are in particular the collection of Ottoman measuring instruments as well as ceramics, calligraphies and tiles. Works by European artists from the 17th to

the 19th centuries are also showcased here. Changing temporary exhibitions are dedicated to contemporary art.

8 Çukurcuma This small district around the Çukurcuma Caddesi is one of the oldest areas in Beyoglu. In earlier times, warehouses and factories dominated in the area, but in the last few decades Çukurcuma has undergone a massive change, and many galleries, furniture and antique stores have created an entirely different ambience. You may discover many a precious find when browsing through the stores. In addition, the district also has some pleasant cafés that invite you to linger.

9 Taksim This square is a major traffic hub, with several main streets and bus lines meeting here. It is also the turning point for the nostalgic

tramway coming up from the Istiklal Caddesi. The traffic junction is fringed by theaters and movie houses, hotels and street stalls, restaurants and bars, making it one of the busiest places in town.

SHOPPING

1 Antikart The jewelry shop is one of several housed in a shopping arcade. On sale are impressive replicas of ancient silver jewelry from Anatolia. The prices are mostly within an acceptable range.
Istiklal Caddesi 207,
Tel + 90 (0) 212 252 44 82,
Mon–Sat 10.00–21.30,
Sun 12.00–21.30.

2 Galatasaray Fish Market Istanbul boasts a number of different fish markets, but that in Galatasaray is one of the most traditional ones. The fishmongers always have a great

THE HIGHLIGHTS OF BEYOĞLU

At the Leb-i derya you can enjoy delicious food as well as sepctacular views of the Bosphorus.

selection of fresh fish on offer. Cheese and even candies can also be bought at the market.
Galatasaray,
daily till late at night

3 **Mavi Jeans** This is the place for trendy jeans by famous designer brands. Aside from trousers, Mavi Jeans also has a range of sweat shirts, T-shirts and jackets from different producers, in many different colors and styles.
Istiklal Caddesi 117,
www.mavi.com,
9.30–21.00 daily.

EATING AND DRINKING

4 **Leb-i derya** The minimalist decor is characteristic for this restaurant. Other key features are an excellent service and fabulous views of the Bosphorus. But the main reason to visit is the perfect way in which the food is prepared here. The cuisine is predominantly Mediterranean: the menu features fish dishes as well as pasta and risotto.
Istiklal Caddesi 227,
Tel +90 (0) 212 243 43 75,
www.lebiderya.com,
Mon–Thu 11.00–2.00,
Fri 11.00–3.00, Sat 10.00–3.00,
Sun 10.00–2.00.

5 **Chez Vous** Diners seek out this eatery not only for the quality of the food but also in order to see and be seen. The restaurant features modern design, and the mainstay of the menu are delicious snacks and light salads.
Firuzaga Mahallesi
Cezayir Sokak 21,
Tel +90 (0)212 245 95 32.

6 **360° Instanbul** Opened as recently as 2006, the restaurant has already received several awards – and not only because of the superb, panoramic views that can be enjoyed here, as is indicated by the name. The cuisine presents a mixture of international dishes, all refined with an unmistakable Turkish touch, making each meal exciting. And of course it also has a range of suitable wines to match.
Istiklal Caddesi 311,
Tel +90 (0) 212 251 10 42,
www.360istanbul.com,
Sun–Thu 12.00–1.00,
Fri, Sat 12.00–3.00.

7 **Changa** Much – but not everything here – revolves around fish. Diners may watch the chefs during their food preparation through a glass floor, so no secrets there then! Walls and ceilings are handpainted, and tables and chairs were created by designers.
Siraselviler Caddesi 47,
Tel +90 (0) 212 251 70 64,
www.changa-istanbul.com,
Mon–Sat 18.00–1.00.

NOTES